THE
NORTHWEST GOLFER
Washington Edition

**A guide to every golf course
where the public is welcome
in the state of Washington**

**By
KiKi Canniff**

Artwork & Photographs

All photos and artwork within each golf course listing was supplied by the golf course and is their property.

Cover Design

Heather Kibbey - Northwest Publishers Consortium - Lake Oswego, OR - www.NPCBooks.com

Publisher

One More Press - P.O. Box 21582 - Keizer, OR 97307 - www.OneMorePress.com

ISBN: 978-0-941361-460

TABLE OF CONTENTS

INTRODUCTION

This book provides details on every public golf course located in the state of Washington. Besides public courses, it also includes all of the region's semi-private courses that provide regularly scheduled times for public play. In all, The Northwest Golfer; Washington Edition, describes 198 golf course locations; some offer more than one course, bringing that total count to 215.

Unless you're looking for membership in a private club, this is the only guide a Washington golfer will need. It is also available in eBook format, so golfers can store it on their cell phone or laptop. That way, no matter where a golfer travels in Washington, they can always find the closest course. A quick reference line at the beginning of each course listing lets you instantly determine if a course is right for your schedule and budget.

How To Use The Northwest Golfer

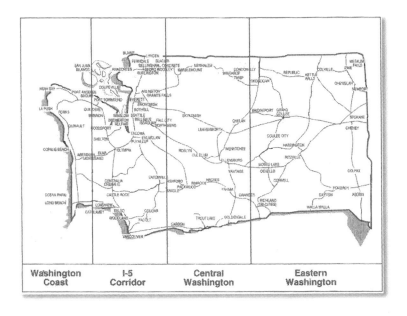

| Washington Coast | I-5 Corridor | Central Washington | Eastern Washington |

This edition covers all of Washington's courses; a separate volume provides full details on Oregon's courses. This book begins with a brief introduction, and a map showing how the state has been divided into four regions: Coast, I-5 Corridor, Central, and Eastern Washington. In the book, each region has its own section.

Every section begins with a map of the region; every town with a golf course open to the public appears on that map. Listings for the cities and their golf courses follow.

What You'll Find In Each Course Listing

Throughout this book, course listings begin with complete contact information. This is where you'll find the name of the course, its location, website link (if available), and reservation or pro shop phone number.

Right below the course name you'll find a quick reference information line highlighting the number of holes available, total yardage from the longest tees, men's par, and price category.

The price category is defined by one to five dollar signs. A single dollar sign calls your attention to a bargain course, two shows it is moderately priced, three denotes a higher-priced course, four is expensive, and five denotes a deluxe or super-expensive golf course.

The actual dollar amounts used to categorize the courses is based on the rate available to all golfers. On an expensive course it could indicate off-season or twilight rates. Prices could be higher during peak schedules.

The exact breakdown is as follows:

$ - Under $20.00

$$ - $20.00 to $40.00

$$$ - $40.01 to $99.99

$$$$ - $100.00 - $199.99

$$$$$ - $200.00 and over

Once you have determined that a course fits your needs, read the full listing and you'll learn what the terrain is like, when it is open, whether or not they take reservations, and what makes that particular course special.

You'll find out exactly how much they charge for green fees and rental equipment, whether or not they have discount days or times when everyone can play for reduced fees, the women's par, and if juniors or seniors can play for discounted rates. Unless otherwise noted, junior rates are for those 17 and under; senior rates are for golfers 65 and older.

Facilities are also described. If the course has a putting green, driving range, practice area, or offers lessons, this book lets you know. It will tell you whether you'll find a snack bar, restaurant, lounge, or overnight accommodations too. And, you'll learn if they offer banquet facilities, serve alcohol, or provide help with tournament planning.

At the end of each listing you'll find concise, easy-to-follow directions.

Locating A Favorite Course

To locate all of the golf courses in a particular city quickly, go to the region where that city is located; the cities are then listed alphabetically, and all courses found in or near that city follow.

In the index you will find every course listed by golf course name, allowing you to instantly locate any course you already know by name. The index also includes city page numbers and groupings by cost, course length, and important features.

The author has made every effort to include all of the state's public and semi-private courses, and has worked with the staff at each course to provide accurate information.

The Northwest Golfer has been around since 1987. This edition has been completely updated, and all of the state's new public courses have been added. The book has been broken into two volumes; one for Washington and another for Oregon.

AN INTRODUCTION TO WASHINGTON GOLF COURSES

Washington has more than two hundred public and semi-private golf courses that offer regular public hours.

One of these locations provides two 18-hole golf courses plus one 9-hole golf course; 45 holes all total. Four locations have 36 holes - two 18-hole golf courses, five locations sport 27 holes - three 9-hole courses, and three locations house an 18-hole championship course plus a 9-hole course.

Nearly all of the multi-course sites are found in and near the I-5 Corridor.

Course designers include Arnold Palmer, Bunny Mason, Robert Muir Graves, Robert Trent Jones, Mike Asmundson, Peter Jacobsen, Chandler Egan, Robert Cupp, William Overdorf, John Harbottle, Bob Tachell, Jack Frei, John Fought, and many others. Washington's natural terrain attracts some of golf's best course architects.

Nearly two dozen older Washington courses are still in use; built prior to 1940, most have seen one or more redesigns. Mature landscape and historic buildings are often the only sign that you're playing an 80-year-old course.

Washington golfers often see wildlife on the course. At the Leavenworth Golf Club an occasional bear is spotted; elk and deer visit Cathlamet's Skyline Golf Course, and deer and coyote are regularly sighted at both Stanwood's Kayak Point and Woodinville's Wellington Hills. At the Carnation Golf Club you may see bald eagles as well as deer on the course.

Some Washington golf courses offer unbeatable views. You can golf within sight of Mount St. Helens, in the shadow of Mt. Rainier and Mt Adams, in view of the San Juan Islands and the Strait of Juan de Fuca, along the Olympic and Cascade Mountain Ranges, beside the Columbia River Gorge, in a high alpine desert, next to raging rivers, and other scenic places.

With 198 separate courses and 215 individual 9-hole and 18-hole courses everyone can find lots of places perfect for their skill level and budget. So, why not join that exclusive group of golfers who can honestly say …

"I've golfed every course in Washington!"

Note: Most fees quoted do not include Washington sales tax.

Region One
The Washington Coast

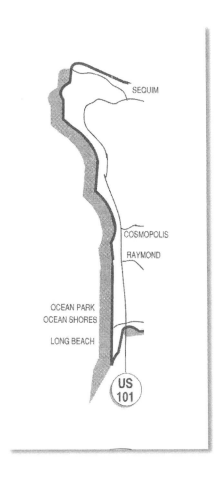

COURSES AT OR NEAR THE WASHINGTON COAST

The coastal region includes the west side of the Washington Olympic Mountains as well as all of the land that lies between those tree-covered mountains and the Pacific Ocean.

Only six cities in this region have public golf courses. Those courses are found in Cosmopolis, Long Beach, Ocean Park, Ocean Shores, Raymond and Sequim; Sequim has two public courses but the other five cities have only one each.

Ocean Park's Surfside Golf Course sits right on the ocean, as does the Peninsula Golf Course in Long Beach. The Peninsula course overlooks the Graveyard of the Pacific, a treacherous place where hundreds of ships have been wrecked and sunk during the past 150 years.

At 6610 yards, The Cedars at Dungeness in Sequim is the longest 18-hole golf course in this area, and a great winter course as well. Both The Cedars, and Sequim's second course Sunland, have views out into the Strait of Juan de Fuca from their fairways making them both beautiful courses to play on a sunny day.

The Willapa Harbor Golf Course in Raymond is the oldest coastal course in the state of Washington. Built in 1926, at 3004 yards it is also the longest 9-hole course in this region.

The following cities at or near the Washington Coast have golf courses open to the public.

Cosmopolis	Long Beach
Ocean Park	Ocean Shores
Raymond	Sequim

Cosmopolis

Highland Golf Course

18 Holes ◇ Par 70
Length 6112 yards ◇ $-$$

2200 First Street
Cosmopolis, WA

360-612-3432
Reservations Recommended

Open year round, Highland was built in 1929. A second nine holes were added in 1994. The course has a park-like look with bent grass greens and a gently rolling terrain. You'll find three tees at every hole allowing for variety. Designed by William Overdorf, the slope is 111 and the course rating 68.1. The women's par is 71 for a total distance of 5165 yards.

Green fees seven days a week are $15 for 9 holes or $25 for 18. Seniors and active military members can play 9 holes for $12 or 18 for $22. Juniors play for $7.50 and $14. Clubs rent for $10, pull carts are $5 and motorized carts are $14 for 9 holes or $24 for 18.

Facilities include a putting green, chipping area, a snack bar that serves cold beer, a driving range and a full-service pro shop where you can get help with tournament planning and schedule lessons. At the driving range you'll find a covered area offering both mat and grass tees. You can get a bucket of balls for $5-10 depending on how many you need.

Directions: The Highland Golf Course is located right in Cosmopolis. Simply leave Highway 101 south of Aberdeen and drive to First Street.

Long Beach

Peninsula Golf Course

9 Holes ◇ Par 33 ◇ Length 2148 yards ◇ $-$$
9604 Pacific Way ◇ Long Beach, WA
360-642-2828 ◇ Reservations Advised
www.peninsulagolfcourse.com

Built in 1947, this 55 acre Scottish-type course is fairly flat with only a few slight hills. It's a good test of skills for most golfers. Open year round from 8:00 am to 7:00 pm. Two sets of tees are available adding challenge to an 18-hole game.

Located near the Graveyard of the Pacific, a place where hundreds of ships have sunk, each hole has been named for a lost vessel. The 1st hole is one of the most difficult covering 313 yards over undulating fairways, the 6th and 7th holes have a waterway crossing the fairway, and the 8th hole has trees with a pond waiting behind for errant balls.

During the summer season which runs thru September you'll pay $18 for 9 holes or $25 for 18 all week long. After 4:00 pm everyone plays for $15 for 9 holes or $20 for all you can play.

Seniors and active military can play for $16 and $23. On Monday, Tuesday and Wednesday senior can play all day for $16. You can rent clubs for $7.50. Juniors pay $5. Pull carts rent for $2 and power carts are $12 for 9 holes or $18 for 18 holes.

Facilities include a snack bar, putting green and limited pro shop. The staff can help with tournament planning and they offer golf lessons.

Directions: Located just north of the Long Beach city limits.

Ocean Park

Surfside Golf Course

9 Holes ◇ Par 36 ◇ Length 2960 yards ◇ $-$$

31508 "J" Place ◇ Ocean Park, WA

360-665-4148 ◇ Reservations Recommended

www.surfsidegolfcourse.com

Surfside was built in 1968 and remains open year round from 7:00 am to dusk. This is a fairly level course right on the ocean. Two sets of tees allow you to play 18 holes with a total length of 6065 yards. The distance from the ladies' tees is 5605 yards for 18 holes or 2788 yards for 9 holes.

Green fees remain the same seven days a week, $20 for 9 holes or $35 for 18. Seniors can Monday thru Thursday for $17 and $30. Juniors pay $10 for 9 holes Monday thru Thursday.

Clubs rent for $10 and $15, handcarts are $3-5 and motorized carts $16 and $32.

You'll find a full-service pro shop offering help with tournament planning and lessons plus a driving range and a snack bar that sells beer. The driving range is for irons and a bucket of balls will cost you $2-5.

Directions: The Surfside Golf Course is located north of Ocean Park; simply follow the signs.

Ocean Shores

Ocean Shores Golf Course

18 Holes ◇ Par 71 ◇ Length 6252 yards ◇ $-$$

500 Canal Drive NE ◇ Ocean Shores, WA

360-289-3357

www.oceanshoresgolf.com

Ocean Shores began as a 6-hole course. It now sports 18 holes and is open year round. The greens are fast and the fairways fairly flat and lined with fir, cedar and hemlock trees. The back nine winds through what remains of a spruce forest. The front nine is a links-style course. The women's tees have a total distance of 5173 yards for par 72. With the Grand Canal cutting through the course and wetlands touching most of the last 9 holes nature presents plenty of hazards.

Summer green fees April thru September are $27 for 9 holes or $45 for 18 on weekends and holidays. Weekdays it's $25 and $40. At Twilight it's $25. Seniors play for $20 and $32. Juniors are $20 for 9 or 18. The rest of the year it's $20 and $32 on weekends and holidays or $18 and $30 during the week. Seniors pay $16 and $25. Clubs rent for $10 and $15, pull carts are $5, and motorized carts $16 and $28. Bring your own cart and the trail fee is $5 for 9 holes or $7.50 for 18.

Facilities include a full-service pro shop, clubhouse and a practice range. At the snack bar you'll find sandwiches, beer and wine. At the driving range you can get a bucket of balls for $4. Both grass and mat tees are available.

Directions: Ocean Shores Golf Course is located on Canal Drive, right in Ocean Shores.

Raymond

Willapa Harbor Golf Course

9 Holes ◇ Par 36 ◇ Length 3004 yards ◇ $-$$

2424 Fowler Road ◇ Raymond, WA

360-942-2392 ◇ Reservations Available

www.willapaharborgolfandrv.com

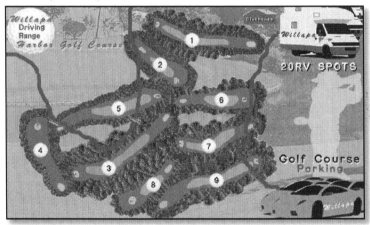

The South Fork River winds its way through the Willapa Harbor course, in fact it snakes through twice on one hole. The fairways are flat with gentle slopes, edged by trees and many have water hazards.

Built in 1926 this is coastal Washington's oldest golf course. It is also the longest 9-hole course in this region. Open year round it offers four tees per hole. The slope is 119 and the ratings 68.8 for men or 72.7 for women. The total distance for women is 2878 yards.

You can play 9 holes for $16 or 18 holes for $26 all week long. Seniors pay $13 for 9 holes or $21 for 18. The same rates are available for active military members. Twilight rates begin at 4:00 pm when rates drop to $12 for 9 holes or $20 for 18. Clubs are $8 and $13, handcarts $3 and $5 and motorized carts $16 and $26.

Facilities include a snack bar where you can get hot sandwiches and cold beer or wine plus a full-service pro shop and driving range. At the range you'll find both grass and mat tees and will pay $4 for a small bucket of balls or $7 for a large bucket. Help with tournament planning and lessons are available. This course also has a 20-space RV camp with hookups.

Directions: Leave Highway 101 on Fowler Street and follow to course.

Sequim

The Cedars at Dungeness

18 Holes ◇ Par 72 ◇ Length 6610 yards ◇ $-$$

1965 Woodcock Road ◇ Sequim, WA

360-683-6344 ◇ Reservations Advised

www.7cedarsresort.com

The Strait of Juan de Fuca is visible from The Cedars 7th tee and the course includes a sand bunker on the 3rd hole that's shaped like a crab. This is a great winter course and relatively flat and easy to walk. Built in 1969, this is coastal Washington's longest 18-hole course. The women's tees have a total distance of 6063 yards. The course rating is 70.2 and the slope 125 for men or 73.7 and 127 for women.

Green fees May thru September are $22 for 9 holes or $40 for 18 Monday thru Thursday, $24 and $47 the rest of the week. During March, April and October rates are $20 and $35 during the early week or $35 to $40 Friday thru Sunday. The balance of the year you'll pay $17-18 for 9 holes or $30 for 18. Motorized carts are $13 per person for 9 holes or $17 per person for 18. Pull carts rent for $4-6 and clubs are $15-25.

Facilities include a restaurant/lounge with a liquor license plus a driving range, banquet area and full-service pro shop. At the range you can get a bucket of balls for $4-8. Lessons and help with tournament planning are available.

Directions: To reach The Cedars course head south on Sequim Avenue to Woodcock Road, turn left and drive 3 miles.

Sunland Golf & Country Club

18 Holes ◇ Par 72 ◇ Length 6066 yards ◇ $-$$

109 Hilltop Drive ◇ Sequim, WA

360-683-6800 ◇ Reservations Required

www.sunlandgolf.com

This semi-private course has a fairly flat terrain and a fantastic view of the Olympic Mountains as well as the Strait of Juan de Fuca. Designed by Ken Putnam, it opened in 1972.

The greens are fast, the fairways narrow and tree lined and they have two sets of tees. There are lots of sand bunkers and the distance from the women's tees is 5567 yards for a par of 73. The course rating is 70.4 and the slope 120.

Summer rates May thru October are $19 for 9 holes or $35 for 18. Juniors play for $10 and $14. Twilight rates start at 2:00 pm and are $14 and $25 for everyone. Winter green fees are $15 and $27 for adults. Electric carts rent for $8 per seat per 9 holes or $15 for 18 and hand carts rent for $5.

They have a putting green, chipping area, full-service pro shop, driving range and a snack bar that offers cold beer. Help with tournament planning and lessons are available.

Directions: To find the Sunland Golf & Country Club course leave Highway 101 on Sequim-Dungeness Way, and head north for 3 miles.

Region Two
The Washington I-5 Corridor

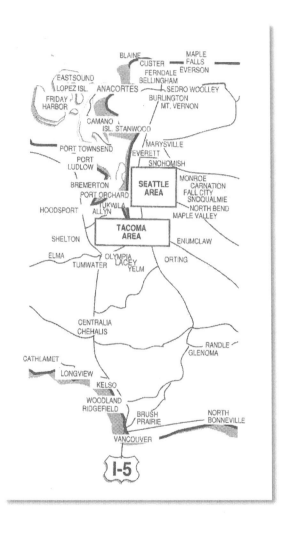

COURSES IN AND NEAR WASHINGTON'S I-5 CORRIDOR

This region has many multiple golf course sites. The largest, Willows Run Golf Club in Redmond. offers 45 holes. They have two 18-hole courses Coyote Creek and Eagle's Talon plus a 9-hole course Heron Links. They also have a miniature 18-hole putting course.

You'll find double 18's in Blaine, Bremerton, Lacey and Bellevue, Washington. Blaine's Semi-ah-moo Resort has two 18-hole courses open to the public on alternate days; allowing for public play seven days a week. Gold Mountain, in Bremerton, has the 7104 yard Olympic course plus the Cascade course at 6707 yards. The Golf Club at Hawks Prairie opened their 18-hole Woodlands course in 1995 and added the 18-hole Links course in 1999. South of Bellevue, in Newcastle, two Robert Cupp designed courses, Coal Creek and China Creek, are open for public play.

Triple nine-hole courses are found in Burlington, Chehalis, Port Ludlow, Fort Lewis and Puyallup. In Kent and Tacoma you'll find courses with a combination of both 9 and 18 holes.

With land disappearing fast, courses in this region are being created out of old farms, ranches and forests. Lam's Golf Links in Oak Harbor was once a poultry farm, Raspberry Ridge in Everson sprang out of a berry farm, Blue Boy West in Monroe an old horse farm and Puyallup's Lapoma Firs was once a Christmas tree farm. The North Bellingham Golf Course was built on the historic Wilder Ranch, both the Lake Spanaway and Discovery Bay courses were carved from the forest and Kelso's Three Rivers Golf Course is built atop Mount St. Helens volcanic ash.

And, there are plenty of 7000+ yard courses in the I-5 region. You'll find them in Auburn, DuPont, Bothell, Port Orchard, Shelton, Tacoma and Tumwater. These courses range from 7038 to 7585 yards in length; the longest is in Tacoma and the newest in DuPont.

The Seattle Area includes Bainbridge Island, Bellevue, Bothell, Clinton, Kent, Lynnwood, Mountlake Terrace, Redmond, Renton and Seattle. The Tacoma Area includes the cities of Auburn, DuPont, Fort Lewis, Gig Harbor, Puyallup, Spanaway, Sumner, Tacoma and Union.

The following cities in Washington's I-5 Corridor have golf courses.

Allyn	Anacortes
Arlington	Auburn (Tacoma Area)
Bainbridge Island (Seattle Area)	Bellevue (Seattle Area)
Bellingham	Blaine

Bothell (Seattle Area)

Brush Prairie

Camano Island

Cathlamet

Clinton (Seattle Area)

DuPont (Tacoma Area)

Elma

Everett

Fall City

Friday Harbor

Glenoma

Kelso

Lacey

Lopez Island

Maple Valley

Monroe

Mt. Vernon

North Bonneville

Orting

Port Orchard

Puyallup (Tacoma Area)

Redmond (Seattle Area)

Ridgefield

Sedro Woolley

Snohomish

Spanaway (Tacoma Area)

Sumner (Tacoma Area)

Tukwila

Union (Tacoma Area)

Woodland

Bremerton

Burlington

Carnation

Chehalis

Custer

Eastsound

Enumclaw

Everson

Fort Lewis (Tacoma Area)

Gig Harbor (Tacoma Area)

Hoodsport

Kent (Seattle Area)

Longview

Lynnwood (Seattle Area)

Marysville

Mountlake Terrace (Seattle Area)

North Bend

Olympia

Port Ludlow

Port Townsend

Randle

Renton (Seattle Area)

Seattle (Seattle Area)

Shelton

Snoqualmie

Stanwood

Tacoma (Tacoma Area)

Tumwater

Vancouver

Yelm

Allyn

Lakeland Village Golf Course

27 Holes ◇ Par 71 ◇ Length 5724 yards ◇ $-$$

E 200 Old Ranch Road ◇ Allyn, WA

360-275-6100 ◇ Reservations Recommended

Lakeland sports three 9-hole golf courses. Each is surrounded by homes. The view from here includes Mt. Rainier, the Olympic Mountains and Puget Sound's Case Inlet. Designed by Bunny Mason this semi-private course was built in 1972 and is part of a residential community. The course has lots of ponds and bunkers, is fairly flat and open year round from sunrise to sunset. The slope is 117 and the course rating 68.5. From the women's tees the distance is 4925 yards for par 72.

On weekends you'll pay $25 for 9 holes or $40 for 18. On Mondays it's $20 and $30, $15 and $22 after 12:00 pm on Tuesdays and Wednesdays, $20 and $30 on Thursdays and $20 and $35 on Fridays.

Twilight rates begin at 3:00 pm when everyone plays for $15 and $22. On Monday and Tuesday seniors can play for $15 and $22. The junior rate is $12 and $18 all week long. All active military members receive a 20% discount. Motorized carts are available, they rent for $18 when playing 9 holes or $30 for 18.

Facilities include a practice bunker, chipping green, a nice restaurant and lounge, pro shop, espresso bar, clubhouse and driving range. Lessons and help with tournament planning are available.

Directions: Located on Highway 3, just before you get to Allyn take Lakeland Drive up the hill.

Anacortes

Gallery Golf Course
18 Holes ⬦ Par 70 ⬦ Length 6351 yards ⬦ $-$$

3065 N Cowpens Road ⬦ Oak Harbor, WA

360-257-2178 ⬦ Reservations Available

www.navylifepnw.com/programs/3fa43e97-345b-4238-bfc4-3b3a1d7d937a

Gallery is part of the Navy Golf Program, but open for public play with reservations. You'll encounter some sand, water on five holes, small trees and an easy-to-walk terrain. The front nine is flat and the back nine has some hills.

Built in 1948, a view of Puget Sound and distant snow-capped mountains make it a pretty place to play. Open daily from dawn to dusk, the slope is 121 and the course rating 70.1. This course is well maintained and the greens small and fast.

Green fees vary. Active duty and retired military pay $10.50 for 9 holes or $18.50 for 18 during the winter or $15.50 and $23.50 in summer.

Department of Defense employees summer rate is $19.50 or $20.50. In winter they pay $13.50 or $24.50. Guests pays $16.50 for 9 holes during the winter or $30.50 for 18. In the summer they pay $25.50 or $35.50.

Twilight rates are only available May thru September, begin at 4:00 pm and you can play until dusk for $24.

Golf clubs rent for $7-25 depending on number of clubs and quality, pull carts are $5 and motorized carts $14 per person for 9 holes or $27 for two playing 18. Bring your own cart and the trail fee is $9.

Facilities include putting and practice greens, a full-service pro shop, a deli with hot lunch and cold beer and a 25-tee grass driving range. You can sign up for golf clinics and lessons at the pro shop.

On the driving range tokens are $3 each.

Directions: Located about 20 miles south of Anacortes; follow Highway 20 west 17.2 miles and turn right on Ault Field Road. Take this .8 mile to Clover Valley Road, turn right, go .2 mile to N. Cowpens Road and course.

Lam's Golf Links

9 Holes ◇ Par 28 ◇ Length 1151 yards ◇ $

597 Ducken Road ◇ Oak Harbor, WA

360-675-3412 ◇ Reservations Available

www.lamsgolflinks.com

This course has four ponds affecting over half the holes. Trees and natural roughs keep the rest interesting. A family-owned par 3, it has been operating since 1972. This was once a poultry farm surrounded by grain fields.

Green fees during the week are $7 for 9 holes or $10 for 18. On weekends and holidays you'll pay $10 or $14. Seniors and children age 8 and younger can play for $5 and $7 Monday thru Friday except on holidays. Golf clubs and pull carts rent for $3 each. They hold weekly golf tournaments for anyone wishing to sign up. The fee is $10 in advance.

Facilities include a clubhouse with a small pro shop. They also have an 18-hole miniature golf course that is simple but fun for the kids.

Directions: Located near Deception Pass State Park. From Anacortes take Highway 20 south for 11 miles and turn left onto Ducken Road.

SWINOMISH CASINO GOLF LINKS

18 Holes ◇ Par 72 ◇ Length 6177 yards ◇ $-$$

12518 Christianson Road ◇ Anacortes, WA

360-293-3444 ◇ Reservations Available

www.swinomishcasinoandlodge.com/golf/the-course

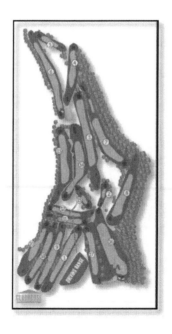

This year-round golf course is surrounded by trees and the terrain is a combination of flat and hilly. Designed by Rod Turner it first opened in 1945. The slope is 110 and the rating 68.4. The layout is tight and they have 3 ponds to gobble up your balls. Par from the forward tees is 74 for a total distance of 5788 yards. Formerly known as Similk Golf Course it is open from dawn to dusk during peak season. In the winter they open at 8:00 am.

Green fees on weekends and holidays are $20 for 9 holes or $33 for 18. On weekdays it costs $17 or $28. Juniors play for $10 and $15 all week. Twilight rates begin at 4:00 pm when everyone plays for $20 on weekdays or $25 on weekends. Clubs rents for $25, pull carts $5 and motorized carts are $8 and $13 for 2 people.

Facilities include a putting green, snack shop, banquet room, 11-tee driving range and a limited pro shop. You can get help with tournament planning at the pro shop. At the driving range you'll pay $4-12 for a bucket of balls.

Directions: Located 4.6 miles southeast of downtown. Follow Highway 20 to the golf course road. Watch for signs as you round the first bay inlet.

Arlington

Gleneagle Golf Course

18 Holes ◇ Par 70 ◇ Length 5851 yards ◇ $-$$

7619 Country Club Drive ◇ Arlington, WA

360-435-6713 ◇ Reservations Available

www.gleneaglegc.com

31

You'll find plenty of sand and water at Gleneagle. It's a good place for golfers of all levels of skills. This target-style course offers four sets of tees. From the forward tees the total distance is 5050 yards. From the back tees the slope is 140 and the course rating 75.5.

Tall trees, water and sand plus well designed fairways make this an interesting place to play. Designed by William Teufel this course opened in 1993.

Green fees Monday thru Thursday are $17 for 9 holes or $25 for 18. Friday thru Sunday you'll pay $20 or $30.

Early birds can play 18 holes for $15 if they get on the course before 8:00 am and the price includes a cart. Twilight rates begin at 4:00 pm, include a cart, and are $25 early in the week or $30 Friday thru Sunday.

Seniors age 55 and older can play Monday thru Thursday for $10 for 9 holes or $17 for 18. Juniors can play for $10 and $17 seven days a week. When fees don't include a cart you can rent one for $8 on 9 holes or $12 for 18.

Facilities include a putting green and practice area and a full-service pro shop where you can get help with tournament planning and sign you up for group or private lessons. The restaurant bar and grill has hot food and cold beer.

They have a driving range that's for irons only. You'll pay $4 for a small bucket of balls or $8 for a large one at the range.

Directions: Located south of downtown Arlington; follow Highway 9 for 2.5 miles and turn right onto Eaglefield Drive. The golf course road is .4 mile down this road; the course is on the left.

Bellingham

Lake Padden Golf Course

18 Holes ◇ Par 72 ◇ Length 6575 yards ◇ $-$$$

4882 Samish Way ◇ Bellingham, WA

360-738-7400 ◇ Reservations Available

www.lakepaddengolf.com

The Lake Padden course was built in 1970 and the setting is gorgeous. Cut out of a forest each hole is separated by thick stands of cedar. The terrain is moderately rolling, the slope 127 and the course rating 71.9. Open year round, summer hours are 6:00 am to dusk but in the winter they don't open until 8:00 am.

They are closed to the public only on Labor Day. You'll find five sets of tees. The total distance from the forward tees is 5458 yards. Golfers younger than age 12 may not play this course if they cannot keep pace with adult golfers.

Green fees include tax and are $20.24 for 9 holes or $33.12 for 18 on weekdays. On weekends you'll pay $41.40 for 18 holes and if 9 holes are available $24.84 for the shorter game. Twilight rates begin at 2:00 pm and are $24.84 for 18 holes during the week and $29.44 on weekends. Twilight rates for 9 holes are available after 6:00 pm and are $16.54 during the week or $20.24 on weekends.

Seniors age 62 and older and juniors age 18 and younger can play 9 holes during the week for $16.56 or 18 for $26.68.

They have a full-service pro shop, two covered driving ranges, putting and chipping practice areas, banquet facilities and a great restaurant and lounge with an outdoor seating area overlooking the course. Private and group lessons as well as golf camps are available.

Directions: Leave I-5 North at exit #246 and follow Samish Way north for 2.3 miles, turning left at the golf course sign. From I-5 south take exit #252, follow Samish Way south 2.6 miles and the signs to the right and the course.

North Bellingham Golf Course

18 Holes ◇ Par 72 ◇ Length 6816 yards ◇ $-$$$

205 West Smith Road. ◇ Bellingham, WA

360-398-8300 ◇ Reservations Available

www.northbellinghamgolf.com

This course opened in 1995 on the historic Wilder Ranch north of Bellingham. The old ranch fields have been used in the design of this Scottish links-style course taking your game through meadows and gently rolling fairways.

A beautiful view of Mt. Baker is seen in the distance. The course rating is 74.0 and the slope 136. Four sets of tees are available. From the forward tees the total distance is 5160 yards.

Monday thru Thursday green fees are $27 for 9 holes or $39 for 18. It's $30 and $44 on Fridays, and on weekends and holidays you'll pay $34 and $49.

Twilight discounts begin at 1:00 pm when fees drop by 20%. At 3:00 pm that discount becomes 40% off regular adult rates. Seniors age 60 and older can play Monday thru Thursday for $34. Juniors age 17 and younger can play 18 holes during the week for $25 or on weekends for $30.

Pull carts rent for $3 for 9 holes or $5 for 18; motorized carts for are $12 per 9 holes or $18. If two riders they're $18 for 9 and $30 for 18.

Facilities include a restaurant and lounge with banquet facilities, a full-service pro shop and a driving range. Private and group lessons are available at the pro shop. They can also help with tournament planning. At the driving range you'll pay $4-7 for a bucket of balls.

Directions: Follow Meridian Street (Highway 539) north of downtown Bellingham 5.4 miles and turn left on West Smith Road.

Sudden Valley Golf Club

18 Holes ◇ Par 72 ◇ Length 6653 yards ◇ $-$$$

4 Clubhouse Circle ◇ Bellingham, WA

360-734-6435 ◇ Reservations Available

www.suddenvalleygolfcourse.com

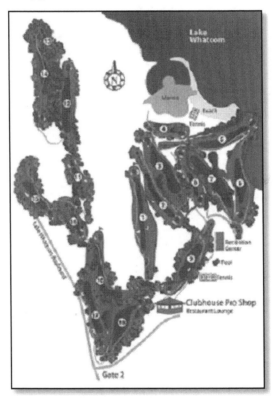

This course overlooks beautiful Lake Whatcom and is well maintained. Designed by Ted Robinson it opened in 1970. The front nine is great for long hitters, open and flat, but you'll need plenty of accuracy to avoid the lakes and creek. The back nine is wooded and hilly with small greens and narrow tree-rimmed fairways. Open year round the slope is 130 and the course rating 71.2. From the forward tees the distance is 5627 yards.

The best rates at Sudden Valley are November thru February when you can play 9 holes for $14 or 18 for $23 Monday thru Thursday. The rest of the week you'll pay $18 and $32. Seniors age 62 and older can play early in the week for $11 and $18. Motorized carts rent for $7 and $10 per rider.

Summer rates are $24 and $42 Monday thru Thursday and $31 and $52 Friday thru Sunday and holidays. Seniors play Monday thru Thursday for $20 and $35.

Facilities include a practice bunker and chipping green, driving range, bar and grill, banquet facilities and a full-service pro shop. Both individual and group lessons are available, as is help with tournament planning. The driving range has grass tees and charges $4-8 for a bucket of balls.

Directions: Leave I-5 North at exit #240 and turn right. Follow this road for about 7 miles to Sudden Valley and turn right at the 2nd gate entrance. From I-5 South take exit #253 and turn left; continue 8 miles and turn left just beyond fire station and left again at the 2nd gate. Signs mark the way.

Blaine

Sea Links Golf Course

9 Holes ◇ Par 29 ◇ Length 1560 yards ◇ $$

7878 Birch Bay Drive ◇ Blaine, WA

360-371-7933

Sea Links was built on the site of the old Birch Bay Golf Resort and is a good place to work on your short game. Designed by John and William Robinson, it first opened in 1984. In 2007 it re-opened with a fresh look. The fairways are open with rolling hills and hazards include several ponds, lots of sand traps and homes along several fairways. It has bent grass greens, a 400' lakeshore. The course rating is 50.7 and the slope 67. From the forward tees the total distance is 1010 yards.

Green fees are $25 on weekdays and $27 on weekends and holidays. Facilities at this executive course include a restaurant and lounge with banquet facilities, a 25-tee driving range, and a full-service pro shop.

Directions: Located on the bay 5.3 miles south of Blaine; take State Highway 548 just 3.7 miles south to Birch Bay/Lynden Road where you will turn right. Follow this 1 mile, turn left onto Harborview Road, left on Birch Bay Drive, and follow this to the golf course.

Semi-ah-moo Resort Golf Course

18 Holes ◇ Par 72 ◇ Length 7005 yards ◇ $$-$$$

8720 Semi-ah-moo Parkway ◇ Blaine, WA

360-371-7015 ◇ Reservations Required

www.semiahmoo.com

Semi-ah-moo Resort is home to two of the state's top public courses. Between the two courses they offer public play seven days a week. The main resort course is open to the public on odd days of the month, challenging, was designed by Arnold Palmer and opened in 1986.

The Trail Golf Course (pictured) was designed by Graham Cooke, opened in 1993, and with its addition the public can play a Semi-ah-moo course seven days a week. One course, Loomis, is open to the public on even days of the month. The resort course is open on odd days of the month. Beautifully landscaped, the greens are fast and true even in the winter. Lakes and a canal snaking thru the course bring water into play on every hole. The course slope is 145 and the rating 75.1.

June thru September Monday thru Thursday green fees are $70 for 18 holes. Friday thru Sunday you'll pay $85. Twilight rates are $55 and $65.

During October, April and May Friday thru Sunday green fees are $55. They're $45 the balance of the week and $35 and $40 at twilight. The biggest bargain is November thru March when everyone pays $35 Monday thru Thursday and $45 the rest of the week.

On the Semi-ah-moo Resort Course the terrain is tree lined, fairly flat with undulating fairways, has water on 5 holes, 67 sand bunkers and five sets of tees. In spring and summer you can golf as early as 6:30 am. The rest of the year the course opens at 8:00 am. From the women's tees the total distance is 5288 yards. The course rating is 73.6 and the slope 130.

June thru September, Monday thru Thursday green fees at either course are $70 for 18 holes. Friday thru Sunday you'll pay $90. Twilight rates are $55 and $65.

During October, April and May Friday thru Sunday green fees are $55. They are $45 the balance of the week and $35 and $40 at twilight. The biggest bargain is November thru March when everyone pays $35 Monday thru Thursday and $45 the rest of the week.

Semi-ah-moo offers overnight resort accommodations, a nice restaurant and lounge with banquet facilities, a full-service pro shop, putting and chipping greens and a 15-tee driving range. At the range you'll find both mat and grass tees and a bucket of balls will cost you $3-5. Lessons and help with tournament planning are available.

Directions: Leave I-5 South at exit #270, turn left onto Birch Bay-Lynden Road, right onto Harborview, and left onto Lincoln Road. From I-5 North take exit #276; head west on Highway 548 following the Drayton Harbor/Harborview Road exit, and turn right on Lincoln Road. Signs will direct you from either exit.

Bremerton

Gold Mountain Golf Club

36 Holes <> Par 72 <> Length 7104 yards <> $$-$$$

105 Country Club Circle <> Tacoma, WA

253-582-8058 <> Reservations Available

www.goldmountaingolf.com

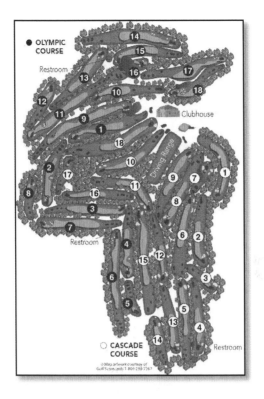

The Gold Mountain Golf Club is owned by the City of Bremerton, open year round, dawn to dusk, and offers some of the state's best golf. There are two 18-hole golf courses at this location. The **Olympic Golf Course** has a slope of 135 and the fairways are wide. The course rating is 74.1 and from the forward tees the distance drops to 5220 yards. Designed by John Harbottle III, this course opened in 1996, has good drainage, four sets of tees, a terrain that varies from flat to rolling hills, lots of trees, some water, plenty of sand bunkers and small greens.

The **Cascade Golf Course** has been open since 1971. Designed by Ken Tyson, the four sets of tees vary from 5306 to 6707 yards. The course par is 71, the slope 120 and course rating 72.1. This is a good course for all levels of players. The two golf courses have adjoining fairways with similar natural features, offer wonderful views of the Olympic Mountains and provide a chance to play near the city, yet surrounded by nature.

Green fees Monday thru Thursday are $36 on the Cascade course or $42 on the Olympic course. On Friday you'll pay $40 or $65 and on weekends and holidays $45 or $70, depending on which course you play. Twilight specials

39

begin at 3:00 pm when rates drop to $25-30 depending on the course and day of the week.

Junior discounts Monday thru Thursday let them play Cascade for $14 or Olympic for $23. Weekend twilight rates for these youngsters are $13 and $19. No matter which course you're playing golf clubs rent for $30 and motorized carts are $16.50 per person. Bring your own cart and the trail fee is $12.

Gold Mountain has practice putting and chipping greens, a large pro shop, a nice restaurant and lounge with banquet facilities and a driving range. Help with tournament planning and lessons are available, ask at the pro shop.

Directions: Follow Highway 3 south to Gorst, follow the signs toward Belfair/Shelton, and at the first stoplight turn right onto Sam Christopherson Avenue. At the stop sign turn left onto W. Belfair Valley Road; the club entrance is 2 miles, on the left.

Rolling Hills Golf Club

18 Holes ◇ Par 70 ◇ Length 5910 yards ◇ $-$$

2485 NE McWilliams Road ◇ Bremerton, WA

360-479-1212 ◇ Reservations Available

Rolling Hills sports a view of snow-capped mountains and is closed only on Christmas Day. The terrain is rolling, water hazards include both a creek and a couple of ponds, and there are plenty of trees and bunkers to keep the game interesting.

This is a pleasant course to walk and offers two sets of tees; from the ladies' tees the distance is 5465 yards. Designed by Don Hogan it opened in 1972. The slope is 115 and the course rating 67.9.

Monday thru Friday you'll pay $20 for 9 holes or $30 for 18. On weekends and holidays it will cost you $22.50 and $33.50. Active military members and golfers younger than 18 or older than 61 can play for $22 on non-holiday weekdays. Twilight rates begin at 2:00 pm and are $24.50 on weekends and holidays and $22 the rest of the week. Motorized carts rent for $18 for 9 holes or $30 for 18. The trail fee to bring your own cart is $10.

They have a restaurant and lounge with banquet facilities, putting greens, chipping and practice areas, a covered driving range and a full-service pro shop. At the driving range you'll find mat tees and can get a bucket of balls for $3-6. Lessons and help with tournament planning are available.

Directions: Located north of downtown; follow Highway 303 for 3.8 miles north, turn right on NE McWilliams, and go another .5 mile to the course.

Brush Prairie

Hartwood Golf Course
9 Holes <> Par 29 <> Length 1588 yards <> $
12506 NE 152nd Avenue <> Brush Prairie, WA
360-896-6041

For a quick game this is a nice course during dry weather. It is wide open and has only a couple of hazards.

Hartwood first opened in 1996 and was designed by Jim and Pat Hart. The views of Mt. Hood and Mount St. Helens add beauty to your game. This course's greens are well maintained and from the forward tees the total distance is 1464 yards.

Green fees are a real bargain at just $14 Friday thru Sunday and $13 the rest of the week. Seniors play for $11 during the week.

Pull carts rent for $2-5 depending on whether you want to push or pull. Facilities include a clubhouse where you'll find light snacks.

Directions: Located 3 miles southeast of town; head east on Highway 503 for 1.3 miles and go right onto NE 152nd Avenue. The course is 1.7 miles further.

The Cedars on Salmon Creek Golf Course

18 Holes ◇ Par 72 ◇ Length 6423 yards ◇ $-$$$

15001 NE 181st Street ◇ Brush Prairie, WA

360-687-4233 ◇ Reservations Available

www.golfcedars.com

This quiet country course opened in 1984, has water hazards on 14 of its 18 holes and no parallel fairways. Open year round it is mostly flat with just two hills, lots of ponds and a year-round creek.

Designed by Jerry James, three sets of tees make it enjoyable for all skill levels. It has fast greens and mature trees. The course drains well making it nice in the winter. The slope is 129 and the course rating 71.2. From the forward tees the total distance is 5216 yards.

Winter green fees begin mid-October and run thru the end of March. You can play 9 holes during the week for $10 or 18 holes for $20. On weekends it's $15 and $25. Seniors age 62 and older and active military members can play any day of the week for $9 per 9 holes. Juniors age 17 and younger can play all week long for $8 and $12.

May thru October rates are $22 for 9 holes during the week or $28 on weekends and holidays. If you play 18 it's $38 and $48. Seniors and military members play 9 for $19 or $33 for 18 during the week and $25 or $43 on weekends and holidays. Juniors pay $5 during the week or $10 weekends.

Golf clubs rent for $10 and $20, pull carts are $3 and $5, and motorized carts are $10 and $15 per seat. Facilities include practice greens, a bar and grill with a banquet area, a pro shop, and a 24-tee driving range. Lessons are available at the pro shop. At the driving range you'll find mat and grass tees and a bucket of balls will cost you $4-8 depending on how many you need.

Directions: Leave I-5 on the 78th Street exit and head east. After this road becomes Padden Parkway you turn left onto NE 152nd Avenue; follow this to the end and turn left on NE 181st Street and follow to the course. From I-205 take the Padden Parkway exit, go east 3.9 miles, turn left onto NE 152nd, follow this to the end, and turn left onto NE 181st Street.

Burlington

Avalon Golf Club

27 Holes ⬦ Par 36 ⬦ Length 3428 yards ⬦ $$-$$$

19345 Kelleher Road ⬦ Burlington, WA

360-757-1900 ⬦ Reservations Available

www.avalonlinks.com

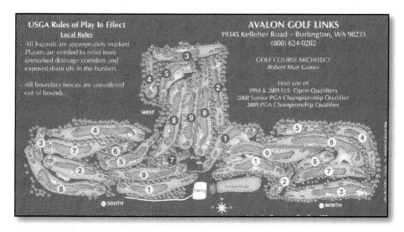

Avalon has three nine-hole courses, spectacular views of the Skagit Valley, gently rolling hills and provides an enjoyable walk. All three courses are par 36, have a slope of 124, a course rating of 72.3 and four sets of tees.

The **West Nine** is the shortest course at 3242 yards. From the forward tees the distance is 2510 yards. The **South Nine** has a total distance from the back tees of 3375 yards and 2808 yards from the forward tees.

The longest course, the **North Nine**, is 3428 yards from the back tees and 2726 from the forward tees. Designed by Robert Muir Graves it was built in 1991.

May thru October, Monday thru Thursday, green fees prior to 11:00 am are $27 and $40. After 11:00 am it's $45 for 18 holes. Twilight rates are $36 for 18 holes. Friday thru Sunday and holidays it's $33 and $50 before 11:00 am or $55 for 18 later. Twilight rates are $45 for 18 holes.

Fall green fees are $20 for 9 holes or $35 for 18 Monday thru Thursday and $26 and $45 Friday thru Sunday and on all holidays. Juniors play for half price and seniors for $18 and $30 Monday thru Thursday except holidays.

Golf clubs rent for $15-35, pull carts $3 and $5, and motorized carts are $10 and $13 per rider. Facilities include a restaurant where beer and wine are available, a huge tournament facility, full-service pro shop and a driving range with grass tees. At the pro shop they can help you with lessons and tournament planning.

Directions: From I-5 northbound take exit #232 and drive to Highway 99, turn left and go another 1.5 miles and turn right onto Kelleher Road. Southbound on I-5 take exit #236 and go to Highway 99; turn right and follow this for 2 miles and turn left onto Kelleher Road. The golf course is .7 mile down Kelleher Road; follow the signs.

Camano Island

Camaloch Golf Course

18 Holes ◇ Par 71 ◇ Length 5807 yards ◇ $$

326 NE Camano Drive ◇ Camano Island, WA

360-387-3084 ◇ Reservations Available

www.camalochgolf.com

Camaloch is relatively flat with just one hill and open year round. You'll find water on several holes and plenty of trees. Located in the Olympic Mountains' rain shadow, the greens are smooth and nicely bunkered.

A second nine was added in 1991. Both the original design and re-design were done by Bill Overdorf. The course slope is 125 and the rating 70. From the forward tees the total distance is 5239 yards.

Peak season green fees are $27 and $33 on weekdays and $30 and $39 on weekends and holidays. Active military members, juniors age 10 to 17 and seniors age 62 and older play for $21 and $26. In the winter weekday rates are $15 and $20. On weekends and holidays you'll pay $18 and $24.

Golf clubs rent for $15, pull carts $3 and motorized carts $14 per rider. Facilities include a snack bar with cold beer, a full pro shop, banquet room, driving range and practice greens. On the range you get 35-40 balls for $5.

Directions: Located 3 miles north on Camano Drive.

Carnation

The Blue Heron Golf Course

18 Holes ◇ Par 71 ◇ Length 6011 yards ◇ $-$$

1810 W Snoqualmie River Road ◇ Carnation, WA

425-333-4151 ◇ Reservations Available

www.theblueherongolf.com

Formerly known as the Carnation Golf Club this course sits in a beautiful valley and is surrounded by the Snoqualmie River. It has mountain views in all directions and golfers often see deer and bald eagles.

Designed by Bob Tachell it opened in 1965. Hazards include lots and lots of water plus trees. The slope is 111 and the course rating 67.7. Open year round, from dawn to dusk, the terrain is flat and easy to walk. From the forward tees the total distance is 4540 yards.

Mid-May thru the first week in October weekday rates are $20 for 9 holes or $35 for 18. Juniors and seniors play for $15 and $25. On weekends everyone pays $25 and $39. The twilight rate begins at 4:00 pm and everyone pays $20. After 6:00 pm it's $15. Those under age 17 play after 5:00 pm for $5.

From mid-March until mid-May it's $18 for 9 holes. They are closed on Mondays and Tuesdays. Kids play free after 12:00 pm when accompanied by a paying adult. Rates are $22 for 9 holes and $30 for 18 in the summer. Golf clubs rent for $10 and $14 and motorized carts are $10 per person.

They have practice greens and bunkers, a restaurant where you'll find cold beer and wine, banquet facilities, a driving range and a full-service pro shop. Tournament planning help and lessons are available at the pro shop.

The driving range is huge and has grass tees. You can get a large bucket of balls for $8 or a small one for $5.

Directions: Located 2.6 miles southwest of downtown. Follow Highway 203 to NE Tolt Hill Road and turn right, go .7 mile and take a left onto West Snoqualmie River Road NE. The course is 1.1 miles further.

Cathlamet

Skyline Golf Course

9 Holes ◇ Par 36 ◇ Length 2433 yards ◇ $

20 Randal Drive ◇ Cathlamet, WA

360-795-8785 ◇ Reservations Available

Skyline's 65 acres offer a great view of the Columbia River from its hillside location. The terrain is hilly with sand traps and a pond. Open year round, elk and deer are often seen on the course. Designed by Ralph Rodahl it is challenging for all levels of players with its ponds and doglegs.

This course is a great bargain at $10 for 9 holes or $15 for 18 holes seven days a week. You can rent golf clubs for $8 and motorized carts are $10 for 9 holes or $15 for 18. They have a limited pro shop where you'll find snacks, beer and help with tournament planning plus a banquet area.

Directions: Located west of town via Highway 4. Follow the highway .9 mile, turn left onto Boege Road, and take the first right onto Clove Street; turn on Randal Drive and follow for .3 mile.

Chehalis

Newaukum Valley Golf Course
27 Holes ◇ Par 36 ◇ Length 2981 yards ◇ $-$$
153 Newaukum Golf Drive ◇ Chehalis, WA
360-748-0461 ◇ Reservations Available
www.newaukumvalleygolf.com

The Newaukum Valley Golf Course has been around since 1979 and is both challenging and pleasant. Open year round, this is a good wet-weather course with its rolling fairways and three 9-hole courses from which to choose.

All three courses have water and sand as well as lots of trees.

The **South Nine Course** will challenge even those with a straight aim. The total distance ranges from 2672 to 2981 yards.

The **East Nine Course** is a little more forgiving unless you get out of bounds. From the back tees the distance is 2853 yards. It is 2440 yards from the forward tees.

The **West Nine Course** is only a par 33 course but it may be the most challenging of all with large trees lining the fairways. From the back tees the distance is 2492 yards and from the forward tees it is 2190 yards.

Green fees Monday thru Friday are $18 for 9 holes or $24 for 18; if you play all 27 holes it will cost you $30. On weekends and holidays you'll pay $22, $30 or $38.

Senior rates begin at age 50. On weekends and holidays seniors pay $20, $25 and $33, the rest of the week $14, $20 and $26. Juniors age 17 and younger play all week long for $10, $15 and $20.

Motorized carts are available and rent for $7 per rider on 9 holes, $12 for 18, or $17 for all 27 holes.

Facilities include a grill serving hot food and cold beer, plus a fully-stocked pro shop offering both private and group lessons.

Directions: Take exit #72 off I-5 North and go left on Rush Road; turn right onto Bishop, right onto Jackson Highway, and drive 2.5 miles to the course.

Riverside Country Club

18 Holes ◇ Par 71 ◇ Length 6155 yards ◇ $-$$

1451 NW Airport Road ◇ Chehalis, WA

360-748-8182 ◇ Reservations Available

www.playriversidegolf.com

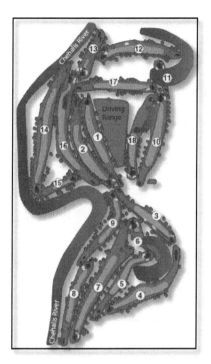

The Chehalis River runs along one side of this course and ponds affect several holes. It is tree lined, fairly level, has white sand bunkers and a beautiful view of Mount St. Helens. The slope is 125 and the ratings 69.7. From the ladies' tees par is 72 for a total distance of 5456 yards. Built in 1927 this is a classic course with mature trees.

On weekends and holidays green fees are $25 for 9 holes or $35 for 18. The rest of the week 9 holes will cost you $19-20 and 18 holes $27-28. Seniors age 60 and older can play 9 holes on weekends for $21 or 18 holes for $30. Weekday senior rates are $16-17 for 9 holes or $21-22 for 18 holes. During the week juniors can play 9 holes for $14, on weekends they pay $17. For 18 holes those rates jump to $19 on weekdays or $23 on weekends and holidays. Motorized carts are available for $20 and $29.

Facilities include a clubhouse with a restaurant/lounge, pro shop, RV park and driving range. At the range you can get a bucket of balls for $5-8. At the pro shop you can arrange for lessons and help with tournament planning.

Directions: From I-5 South take exit #81, head west on Mellen Street, turn left on Airport Road and follow for 2.6 miles. The course will be on right. From I-5 North take exit #77 and head west on Main, turn right on Louisiana Avenue and left on Airport Road. The course is .7 mile on left.

Custer

Dakota Creek Golf Club

18 Holes ◇ Par 71 ◇ Length 5560 yards ◇ $-$$

3258 Haynie Road ◇ Custer, WA

360-366-3131 ◇ Reservations Available

www.dakotacreekgolf.com

This tough little year-round course has grass tees, some hills and is open year round weather permitting. The rating is 67.7, slope 120 and from the forward tees the distance 4505 yards. It started as a 9-hole course running over hilly fields. In 1998 the back 9 was added along the ridge providing more challenge.

The course is open dawn to dusk. When the pro shop is closed deposit your green fees in the lockbox. Wildlife is often spotted on the course.

May thru September rates are $18 for 9 holes and $24 for 18. On weekends and holidays you'll pay $20 and $28. Golf clubs rent for $10 and motorized carts $7 per person per 9 holes. Seniors should ask about discounts. Twilight hours vary but it's cheaper after 2:00 pm and again at 4:00 pm and 6:00 pm. You'll find a limited pro shop and help with tournament planning.

Directions: Leave I-5 at exit #270, follow Valley View Road to its end, and turn right on Haynie Road.

Grandview Club Golf Course

18 Holes ◇ Par 72 ◇ Length 6425 yards ◇ $-$$

7738 Portal Way ◇ Custer, WA

360-366-3947 ◇ Reservations Available

www.golfatgrandview.com

The Grandview course is surprisingly challenging, with its park-like setting, flat terrain, and gorgeous view of Mt. Baker. The slope is 112 and the course rating 70.2. Water comes into play on over half of the holes on this easy-to-walk course. You'll find three sets of tees. From the forward tees the total distance is 5422 yards. Built in 1968 the course is open year round.

During the week adults pay $17 for 9 holes or $26 for 18. On weekends and holidays the rates increase to $19 and $30. After 1:00 pm adults pays $20 and $22. After 2:30 pm it's $18 and $20 and after 4:00 pm $13 and they can play until dusk. Seniors age 60 and older and juniors age 17 and younger can play 9 holes for $16 or pay $24 for 18 holes on non-holiday weekdays.

Golf clubs rent for $10, pull carts $3 and motorized carts are $14 and $22. Bring your own cart and you'll pay $8 for trail fees. You'll find a snack bar offering cold beer and wine and a limited pro shop where you can get help with tournament planning and lessons.

Directions: The course sits between I-5 and Portal Way. From I-5 South take exit #270 and follow the Birch Bay signs 1 mile south to Portal Way and the golf course entry. From I-5 North take exit #266 and head west on Grandview Road until you reach Portal Way. Follow south to the course.

Eastsound

Orcas Island Golf Club

9 Holes <> Par 34 <> Length 2889 yards <> $-$$$

2171 Orcas Road <> Eastsound, WA

360-376-4400 <> Reservations Available

www.golforcas.com

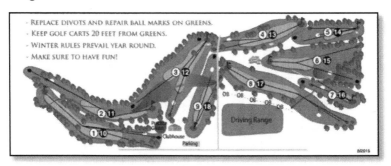

The Orcas Island Golf Club is found in the beautiful San Juan Islands and first opened in 1962. The terrain is a combination of hills and flat areas with bent grass greens, well designed tees and three large ponds. It sits in an evergreen forest and the ponds attract wildfowl as well as golf balls. The course rating is 67.8 and the slope 115.

Once a farm the original farmhouse serves as the clubhouse. Open year round, you'll find four tees. Par from the forward tees is 36 for a distance of 2128 yards. In 2007 this course was purchased by Island residents to avoid its consumption by developers.

May thru September weekend and holiday fees are $33 for 9 holes or $45 for 18. During the week it's $30 and $42. Twilight rates begin at 5:00 pm and you can play until dusk for $25. Juniors age 17 and younger can play for $10 and $15. Off-season green fees for adults are $20 and $25.

Adult golf clubs rent for $15-40, junior clubs $10-15, pull carts $5 and motorized carts $20 for 9 holes or $30 for 18. The clubhouse is not always open November thru March so bring exact change for the drop box.

Facilities include a driving range and a full-service pro shop where you can get help with tournament planning. At the driving range you'll pay $6 for a bucket of balls, $20 for 4 buckets or $40 for 10 buckets.

Directions: Orcas Island is accessible by ferry. From the docks you simply follow Horseshoe Highway 2.5 miles to the golf course.

Elma

Oaksridge Golf Course

18 Holes ◇ Par 70 ◇ Length 5643 yards ◇ $-$$

1052 Monte-Elma Road ◇ Elma, WA

360-482-3511 ◇ Reservations Available

Oaksridge is an easy-to-walk city-owned course situated in a pleasant country setting. The slope is 100 and the course rating 65.3. They are open year round. From the forward tees the total distance is 5423 yards. This course first opened in 1934. The second nine was added in 1975. This course has small greens and a few sand bunkers, plus one pond.

Foursome Fridays are a real bargain at Oaksridge. This rate begins at 2:00 pm and all four players get 9 holes for $20 or 18 for $40. Regular rates are $14 for 9 holes or $24 for 18.

On Tuesdays anyone can play all day for $15, juniors pay $8 and $14 seven days a week and seniors play for $10 and $19.

Golf clubs rent for $5 and motorized carts are $6 and $11 per person.

You'll find a snack bar where you can get cold beer, a small driving range and a full-service pro shop at Oaksridge. Help with tournament planning is available at the pro shop. They also offer group and private lessons.

At the driving range you'll pay $3-5 for a bucket of balls.

Directions: Located west of downtown, 2.3 miles along Monte-Elma Road.

Enumclaw

Enumclaw Golf Course

18 Holes ◇ Par 70 ◇ Length 5561 yards ◇ $-$$

45220 288th SE ◇ Enumclaw, WA

360-825-2827 ◇ Reservations Available

www.golfenumclaw.com

The Enumclaw course is in the foothills of Mt. Rainier and surrounded by trees. This is a picturesque country course with tall trees and rolling hills. The back nine has lots of water. Open year round, the slope is 105 and the course rating 65.9. From the women's tees the total is 5211 yards.

May thru early October weekday green fees are $17 for 9 holes or $25 for 18. On weekends and holidays it's $20 and $32. During the week active military and seniors age 60 and older can play 9 holes for $14 or 18 for $20. Twilight rates are the same for everybody. They're $18 during the week and $21 on weekends. If you want a cart it's $28 or $31.

Juniors age 18 and younger play for $14 and $20 during the week and $17 and $26 on weekends and holidays. Golf clubs rent for $6 and $10, pull carts are $3 and $5, and it's $16 or $28 for motorized carts.

Facilities include a restaurant where you can get hot food and cold beer and a pro shop. At the pro shop you can get help with the tournament planning and sign up for lessons. The restaurant and pro shop were remodeled.

Directions: Located near downtown Enumclaw; follow Roosevelt Avenue (Highway 410) west 1 mile and turn right onto 288th. The course is .2 mile down this road.

Everett

Harbour Pointe Golf Club

18 Holes ◇ Par 72 ◇ Length 6862 yards ◇ $$-$$$

11817 Harbour Pointe Blvd. ◇ Everett, WA

425-355-6060 ◇ Reservations Available

www.harbourpointegolf.com

Harbour Pointe offers a terrific view of Puget Sound from the signature 11th hole where you shoot down a steep ledge toward a postage-stamp-sized green. This course is open year round. The front nine has lots of water, winding its way through wetlands. It was designed by Arthur Hills. The back nine features large evergreens and rolling hills. Harbour Pointe has a course rating of 73.5 and the slope is 147.

Green fees Monday thru Thursday are $57 for 18 holes. Friday thru Sunday and on all holidays you'll pay $72. Early twilight rates begin at 1:00 pm when you play for $47 and $52. Full twilight rates begin at 5:00 pm when you pay $35 and $47.

Facilities include a restaurant and lounge, a 30-tee driving range and a full-service pro shop. Lessons and help with tournament planning are available. At the driving range you'll pay $5 for a small bucket of balls or $9 for a large one.

Directions: Located southwest of town; take Highway 525 to Mukilteo, turn left onto Harbour Pointe Blvd. and go 1.5 miles to the course.

Legion Memorial Golf Course

18 Holes ◇ Par 72 ◇ Length 6900 yards ◇ $$

144 W Marine View Drive ◇ Everett, WA

425-259-4653 ◇ Reservations Available

www.everettgolf.com

This year-round course first opened in 1933, operates from dawn to dusk, and has spectacular views of Puget Sound and the Olympic and Cascade Mountains.

Set in a quiet forest setting, the slope is 128 and the rating 72.8. From the forward tees the total distance is 4805 yards. You'll find three lakes, plenty of sand and trees too.

During the week 9 holes are $26 and 18 holes $35. Weekend rates are $28 and $40. Juniors play during the week for $16. Seniors and active military members pay $27 for 18 holes. November thru February green fees are $22 and $27 on weekdays or $26 and $35 on weekends.

Golf clubs rent for $15, pull carts are $3 and $4, and motorized carts $10 and $15 per rider. The trail fee if you bring your own cart is $8.

The Legion Memorial Golf Course has a clubhouse with banquet facilities and a restaurant where beer and wine is served. They have a practice area and a full-service pro shop where you can sign up for lessons and get help with tournament planning.

Directions: From downtown, follow N Broadway Avenue 3.15 miles north.

Walter E. Hall Memorial Golf Course

18 Holes ◇ Par 72 ◇ Length 6453 yards ◇ $-$$

1226 SW Casino Road ◇ Everett, WA

425-259-4653 ◇ Reservations Available

www.everettgolf.com

Hall Memorial is a reasonably dry winter course and a good place to practice your iron skills as well as putting. You'll find several doglegs, 6 ponds, 5 creeks and large undulating greens. It has four sets of tees, a rating of 69.2 and a slope of 115. The forward tees have a distance of 5219 yards.

During the week 9 holes are $24 and 18 holes $33. Weekend rates are $28 and $38. Juniors play during the week for $16. Seniors and active military members pay $25 for 18 holes. November thru February green fees are $21 and $29 on weekdays, $25 and $32 on weekends.

Golf clubs rent for $15, pull carts are $3 and $4, and motorized carts $10 and $15 per rider. The trail fee when you bring your own cart is $8.

Facilities include a clubhouse, a restaurant serving beer and wine, plus a banquet area and full-service pro shop. Lessons and help with tournament planning are available.

Directions: Located southwest of Everett; take I-5 south to Highway 526. Follow this road 3.6 miles to the course.

Everson

Raspberry Ridge Golf Course

9 Holes ◇ Par 34 ◇ Length 2825 yards ◇ $-$$

6827 Hannegan Road ◇ Everson, WA

360-354-3029 ◇ Reservations Available

www.raspberryridgegc.com

Raspberry Ridge is a year-round course with a fairly flat terrain that is fun and easy to walk. Designed by Bill Overdorf and Bill Robins Sr., this was once a berry farm. The course opened in 1984.

You'll find three sets of tees, large greens, fairly wide fairways and a view of Mt. Baker. The distance from the forward tees is 2335 yards. The rating is 67.3 and the slope 110.

On weekends and holiday you'll pay $16.59 for 9 holes or $23.04 for 18. The rest of the week it's $14.26 and $21.20. Juniors and seniors play for $15.67 and $21.20 weekends and holidays or $13.83 and $19.86 weekdays.

Golf clubs rent for $9.20, pull carts are $2.30 and motorized carts $11.05 and $16.58 for one rider, $16.58 and $23.97 for two. Taxes are included.

Facilities include a limited pro shop and a grill with hot food, and cold beer and wine. At the pro shop you can get help with tournament planning.

The restaurant is open 8:00 am to 4:00 pm seven days a week and has outside seating with a great view of Mt. Baker. It is open only during peak season.

Directions: Located 6.2 miles west of town; take Highway 544 west 6.1 miles to Hannegan Road and turn left to the course.

Fall City

Snoqualmie Falls Golf Course

18 Holes ◇ Par 71 ◇ Length 5465 yards ◇ $-$$

35109 SE Fish Hatchery Road ◇ Fall City, WA

425-392-1276 ◇ Reservations Available

www.snoqualmiefallsgolf.com

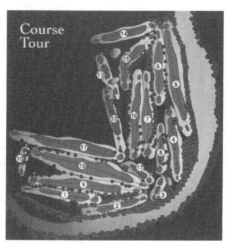

The Snoqualmie Falls Golf Course is situated in the scenic Snoqualmie Valley and is open year round. A few of the fairways parallel the Snoqualmie River. The slope is 102 and the course rating 64.8; from the forward tees the total distance is 5076 yards.

On weekends and holidays you can play 9 holes for $24 or 18 for $36. The rest of the week you can play for $20 and $30. After 3:00 pm seven days a week everyone pays $24 to golf until dusk. On weekdays golfers younger than 18 or older than 61 can play 9 holes for $17 or 18 for $25.

Golf clubs rent for $10 and $15, hand carts $3 and $5, and motorized carts are $9 and $14 per rider. Watch their website for specials.

Facilities include a restaurant/grill that serves cold beer, plus a driving range and full-service pro shop. Private and group lessons, as well as help with tournament planning, are available at the pro shop.

Directions: The Snoqualmie Falls Golf Course road is located .8 mile east of Fall City on Highway 202.

Twin Rivers Golf Course

18 Holes ◇ Par 70 ◇ Length 6074 yards ◇ $-$$

4446 Preston-Fall City Road SE ◇ Fall City, WA

425-222-7575 ◇ Reservations Available

www.twinriversgolfcourse.com

Twin Rivers Golf Course sits at a curve in the Snoqualmie River, nestled between it and the Raging River. Just in case that's not enough water there is a pond in the center of the course. That plus lots of mature trees that will test your aim.

The terrain varies from flat to gently rolling, the mountain views are terrific and wildlife is often spotted. The slope is 109 and the course rating 67.8. From the forward tees the total distance is 4668 yards.

Peak season green fees are $22 for 9 holes or $34 for 18 Monday thru Friday. Juniors and seniors play for $20 and $29. They have a special before 8:00 am when it's $14 and $21 and an afternoon special that runs between 3:00 pm and 5:00 pm of $20 or $29. On weekends and holidays it's $26 and $40 for everyone.

Golf clubs rent for $8 per 9 holes and motorized carts $18 for 9 holes or $28 for 18. Trail fees to bring your own cart are a flat $5. Facilities include a pro shop where you can get help with lessons and tournament planning plus a covered driving range. At the driving range you get 51 balls for $5.

Directions: Located right in Fall City, on the Preston-Fall City Road.

Friday Harbor

San Juan Golf & Country Club

9 Holes ◇ Par 35 ◇ Length 3347 yards ◇ $-$$$

806 Golf Course Road ◇ Friday Harbor, WA

360-378-2254

www.sjgolfclub.com

The San Juan course is relatively flat with some hills, long fairways, small greens and plenty of water. The view is terrific and includes Griffin Bay, Mt. Baker, and other islands in the San Juan Island chain. Built in 1965 this links-style course is open April thru October. It is much tougher than it looks. The slope is 122 and the rating 72.4. From the women's tees the total distance of 3088 yards. Five ponds add excitement to the game.

You'll pay $30 for 9 holes or $45 for 18 May thru September; October thru November, and March thru April, you'll pay $20 and $30. December thru February you'll pay a flat $20. Golf clubs rent for $20 and $30, handcarts $5 and motorized carts are $15 and $25.

Facilities include a restaurant with a full bar, a pro shop and a driving range. At the range a bucket of balls will cost you $3-5. Lessons are available.

Directions: Located on San Juan Island, 3 miles south of Friday Harbor, off Cattle Point Road.

Glenoma

Ironwood Green Golf Course

9 Holes ◇ Par 30 ◇ Length 1512 yards ◇ $

8138 Highway 12 ◇ Glenoma, WA

360-498-5425

Ironwood is a flat executive course with narrow tree-lined fairways and small greens. Built in 1983, it's tougher than you would imagine. Designed by James Redman and open year round, from the women's tees par is 31. The signature hole is #6, where you're required to shoot the creek twice for par 4.

Green fees remain the same seven days a week. You can play 9 holes for $10 or 18 for $15. Golf clubs rent for $3.50, pull carts are $3.50 and motorized carts are $16 for 9 holes or $25 for 18.

Facilities include a putting green, a small RV park and a store where you can get snacks and cold drinks. During the summer they offer golf lessons. Ask at the pro shop.

Directions: Located along Highway 12, in Glenoma.

Hoodsport

Lake Cushman Golf Club

9 Holes ◇ Par 35 ◇ Length 2858 yards ◇ $-$$

210 NW Fairway Drive ◇ Hoodsport, WA

360-877-5505 ◇ Reservations Available

www.lakecushmangolfcourse.com

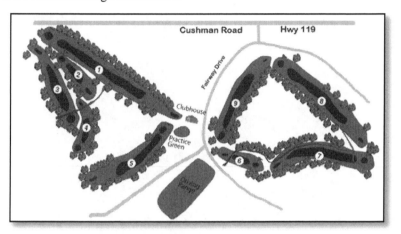

Lake Cushman is open year round unless the rain is really pounding. The terrain is very easy to walk, with lots of trees and a nice view of the mountains. A second set of tees adds enjoyment to playing 18 holes. From the women's tees the total distance is 2682 yards for a par 37. This course first opened in 1967. The course rating is 35.8 and the slope 122.

Green fees during the week are $16 for 9 holes or $25 for 18. On weekends and holidays you'll pay $18 or $27. Juniors can play for $10 and $17 all week long. Twilight rates begin at 3:30 pm. For 9 holes adults pay $10 or $16 for 18. Motorized carts are $10 and $15 per rider.

Facilities include a putting green and chipping area, covered 10-tee driving range, full-service pro shop and a snack bar where you can get cold sandwiches and beer. Tournament help is available at the pro shop. The driving range has mat tees and you can get a bucket of balls for $4, $6 or $8, depending on how many you need.

Directions: Leave downtown Hoodsport on Highway 101, turn left onto Fairway Drive and follow this west 3 miles to the course.

Kelso

Three Rivers Golf Course

18 Holes <> Par 72 <> Length 6648 yards <> $-$$

2222 S River Road <> Kelso, WA

360-423-4653 <> Reservations Available

www.3riversgolfcourse.com

The Three Rivers course was built on Mount St. Helens ash in 1983 and sits beside the Cowlitz River. Owned by the local Elks club, it has good drainage, is playable year round and offers three sets of tees.

You'll find plenty of trees, enough water to keep the game interesting and from the women's tees the total distance is 5368 yards. The course slope is 119.

All week summer green fees are $16 for 9 holes or $30 for 18. Elks Club members pay $12 and $24. Seniors age 62 and older pay $14 for 9 holes or $27 for 18. Juniors age 17 and younger can play for $9 and $15. Twilight specials are for everyone and begin at 2:00 pm. The rate is $12 for 9 holes or $24 for 18.

During the winter everyone pay $12 for 9 holes or $24 for 18.

A motorized cart rents for $7.50 and $15. You'll find a restaurant where you can get cold beer and wine, a driving range and a full-service pro shop. Lessons and help with tournament planning are available at the pro shop.

Directions: Follow River Road South 2.2 miles. Located south of downtown Kelso.

Lacey

The Golf Club at Hawks Prairie

36 Holes ◇ Par 72 ◇ Length 7170 yards ◇ $$-$$$

8383 Vicwood Lane ◇ Lacey, WA

360-455-8383 ◇ Reservations Available

www.hawksprairiegolf.com

Hawks Prairie has two 18-hole golf courses. The **Woodlands Course** has old-growth trees and tees ranging in length from 5600 to 7170 yards. Fairways take you past ponds and wetlands. This course opened in 1995 and has four sets of tees.

The **Links Course** (shown) was built in 1999 and is a Scottish-links-style course. Five sets of tees make this a challenging place to play. Views of Puget Sound and Mt. Rainier make it a beautiful place to play.

Friday thru Sunday and on major holidays it's $47 for an 18-hole game Monday thru Thursday the rate is $36. Twilight rates begin at 5:00 pm when everyone pays $25 Monday thru Thursday or $30 the rest of the week. Seniors who get on the course before 9:00 am pay only $30 Monday thru Thursday.

Rental golf clubs are $50 for a TaylorMade set, pull carts are $5 and motorized carts $15 per seat.

Facilities include putting greens, chipping areas, a bar and grill, pro shop and driving range. At the range you'll find grass and mat tees and pay $5 for a small bucket of balls, $8 for a medium one or $9 for a large bucket.

Directions: Located northeast of downtown. Take I-5 north 2 miles and Highway 510 for 3 miles to Willamette Drive NE, turn right and go 1 mile to Meriwood Drive and turn left. This becomes Vicwood Lane and takes you to the course.

Longview

Mint Valley Golf Course

24 Holes ⬦ Par 71 ⬦ Length 6432 yards ⬦ $-$$

4002 Pennsylvania ⬦ Longview, WA

360-442-5442 ⬦ Reservations Available

www.mint-valley.com

Mint Valley has both a challenging 18-hole course and a short 6-hole par three golf course. You'll find tall trees, well-bunkered greens, lots of water and sand on the 18-hole course. The slope is 127 and the rating 71. The total distance from the forward tees is 5230 yards.

Designed by Ron Fream and built in 1976 it is open year round. The 6-hole course is great for beginners with tees ranging in distance from 50 to 90 yards. This is a good place to tune up your short game or bring new players.

Green fees are $15 for 9 holes and $28 for 18 seven days a week. Happy Hour rates begin at 3:00 pm and green fees are $10 and $20. During the week seniors can play anytime for $15 and $24. Juniors age 9-17 years can play on weekdays for $10 and $18. Carts rent for $16 and $28.

Facilities include a snack bar where you can get cold beer and wine, plus a full-service pro shop and a driving range. At the driving range they offer both mat and grass tees and you get a bucket of balls for $4-6. You can get help with tournament planning and sign up for lessons at the pro shop.

Directions: Take Highway 4 west 2.5 miles, turn right onto 38[th,] and after .7 mile turn left onto Pennsylvania and follow this .2 mile to the course.

Lopez Island

Lopez Island Golf Course

9 Holes ◇ Par 35 ◇ Length 2701 yards ◇ $-$$

589 Airport Road ◇ Lopez Island, WA

360-468-2679

www.lopezislandgolf.com

		1	2	3	4	5	6	7	8	9	Out	10	11	12	13	14	15	16	17	18	In	Tot
Men	Par	3	5	4	3	5	4	4	3	4	35	3	4	4	3	5	4	4	3	4	34	69
Rating 65.4 Slope 106	H'cap	13	15	7	9	3	17	1	11	5		14	2	8	18	6	10	4	12	16		
Yardage	Gold/Blue	147	465	341	132	509	351	369	161	292	2767	140	450	280	120	504	328	339	147	273	2537	5304
Women	Par	3	5	4	3	5	4	4	3	4	35	3	4	4	3	5	4	4	3	4	34	69
Rating 67.0 Slope 108	H'cap	15	7	3	13	1	9	5	17	11		14	6	4	18	2	8	10	16	2		
Yardage	White/Red	140	406	332	126	460	328	339	152	262	2510	129	295	280	114	425	313	274	137	225	2192	4702

Located on an island in the San Juan's, golfers at Lopez Island arrive by ferry, private boat or small plane. The 2900' island airport runway is adjacent to the course and boaters can take a taxi from the docks making it easy to reach. A semi-private course, it is only closed to the public on Tuesday and Thursday prior to 1:00 pm.

The course is open year round April thru September from 9:00 am to 7:00 pm Thursday thru Monday. Many golfers spot deer and rabbits along the narrow fairways. Eagles and hawks often circle above.

Opened in 1958 the terrain is easy to walk with undulating greens. The slope is 106 and the course rating 65.4. From the forward tees the total distance is 2351 yards. Children under age 8 are not permitted on the course.

Green fees May thru October are $20 for 9 holes and $25 for 18 Monday thru Thursday. Friday thru Sunday you'll pay $25 and $35. Twilight rates begin at 4:00 pm and everyone pays $15 to play until dusk. Off-season rates are discounted. Golf clubs can be rented for $7, pull carts are $3, and motorized carts can be reserved – the cost is $20.

Facilities include a practice area, a limited pro shop with a few snack machines and cold drinks, and banquet facilities. They can help with tournament planning at the pro shop.

Directions: Located about 6 miles from the Lopez Island ferry landing; take Fisherman Bay Road to Airport Road and follow this to the course. If you're flying in, the clubhouse is walking distance from the terminal.

Maple Valley

Lake Wilderness Golf Course

18 Holes <> Par 70 <> Length 5409 yards <> $-$$

25400 Witte Road SE <> Maple Valley, WA

425-432-9405 <> Reservations Available

www.lakewildernessgc.com

Maintained by the city of Maple Valley, Lake Wilderness has narrow fairways with lots of water, wetlands, sand and large trees. The terrain is semi-hilly and offers a great view of Mt. Rainier. This demanding course has a slope of 118 and a course rating of 66.1. The total distance from the ladies' tees is 4657 yards. Open year round.

Weekends and holidays you'll pay $36 for an 18-hole game. On weekdays you can play 9 holes for $21 or 18 for $31. If you get on the course before 7:00 am the weekend rate is $26. It is $21 the rest of the week. Twilight rates begin at 3:00 pm and are $22 on weekends or $20 during the week. Juniors can play on weekdays and after noon on weekends and holidays for $10. Seniors pay $21 on non-holiday weekdays and $25 after 11:00 am on weekends. Motorized carts are $8 per seat for 9 holes or $14 for 18.

You'll find a bar and grill with banquet facilities, a full-service pro shop and snack bar. Lessons and help with tournament planning are available.

Directions: Located 1 mile north of downtown Maple Valley; follow Witte Road SE.

Marysville

Battle Creek Golf Course

27 Holes ◇ Par 73 ◇ Length 6600 yards ◇ $-$$

6006 Meridian Avenue N ◇ Marysville, WA

360-659-7931 ◇ Reservations Available

www.battlecreekgolfwa.com

You'll find both an 18-hole regulation course and a 9-hole par 3 course at Battle Creek. The 18-hole course is situated in a scenic wetland area surrounded by fir and pine. This course has a rolling terrain, two large ponds and a nice view of Puget Sound. Designed by Fred Jacobson and built in 1989, the slope is 121 and the course rating 69.5. From the forward tees the total distance is 5286 yards. The 9-hole course covers 1113 yards for a par of 27. Both courses are open year round dawn to dusk. The 9-hole course has a total distance of 1113 yards.

Green fees on the 18-hole course are $19.50 for 9 holes or $31 for 18 on weekdays; on weekends and holidays you'll pay $22 and $38. Seniors, juniors and active military members can play on weekdays for $16.50 and $25. Golf clubs rent for $6 and $10, pull carts $2 and $4, and motorized carts are $7 per rider on weekdays if playing 9 holes, $12-13 per rider for 18 holes. An additional 9 holes will add $4-5. Golf clubs rent for $4 and $6, pull carts $1-2 and motorized carts are $10 and $15.

You'll find a restaurant with banquet facilities where beer and wine are served plus a grass-tee driving range and a full-service pro shop. Lessons and help with tournament planning are available. At the driving range you'll pay $3-5 for a bucket of balls.

Directions: Located west of Marysville. Take State Highway 528 and Marine Drive 3.2 miles to Meridian Avenue and turn right onto course road.

Cedarcrest Municipal Golf Course

18 Holes ◇ Par 70 ◇ Length 5811 yards ◇ $$

6810 84th Street NE ◇ Marysville, WA

360-363-8460

www.cedarcrestgc.com

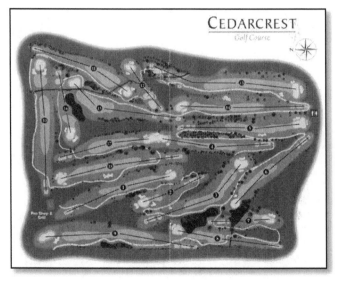

Cedarcrest first opened in 1927 and underwent a major remodel in 1997. You'll find lots of mature evergreens, plenty of natural water features and sand bunkers, as well as small greens. From the forward tees the total distance is 2633 yards. The course slope is 122 and the rating 67.5. Four sets of tees add variety.

On weekends and holidays green fees are $24 for 9 holes or $38 for 18. On weekdays it's $23 and $33. Those over 55 can play during the week for $18 and $26. Anyone can play the Early Bird 18 weekday mornings for $23. On weekends the Early Twilight Rate for 18 is $24 and during the week it's $23. Seven days a week the Late Twilight Rate for 18 is $15.

Motorized carts rent for $9 and $15 per rider. Facilities include a restaurant and lounge with banquet facilities and a pro shop.

Directions: Located east of Marysville. Follow State Highway 528, turn left onto 67th Avenue NE and right onto 84th Street NE. Take this to course.

Monroe

Blue Boy West Golf Course

9 Holes ◇ Par 33 ◇ Length 2200 yards ◇ $-$$

27927 Florence Acres Road ◇ Monroe, WA

360-793-2378 ◇ Reservations Available

www.blueboywest.com

Blue Boy West sits in a mountain setting on an old horse farm; it became a public golf course in 1992. You'll find lots of sand traps, water on 7 holes, some trees and rolling hills.

This is a great place for a quick game and the scenery is nice too. They are open year round and the slope is 109. The course rating is 32.1. This is a great little family course.

On weekends and holidays you'll pay $19 for 9 holes or $25 for 18. The rest of the week it will cost you $18 and $24. Monday thru Friday juniors age 12 and under can play 9 holes for $12 or 18 holes for $16. Seniors and students pay $17 and $23. Pull carts rent for $3, motorized carts are $12 for 9 holes or $22 for 18.

Facilities include a new clubhouse, cafe, banquet area and pro shop. Ask at the pro shop for help with tournament planning.

Directions: Located 6 miles northeast of Monroe; follow Main Street which becomes Old Owen Road staying left at Florence Acres Road. After 3.8 miles you'll come to the golf course.

Mt. Vernon

Eaglemont Golf Club Course

18 Holes ⬥ Par 72

Length 7006 yards ⬥ $$-$$$

4800 Eaglemont Drive
Mt. Vernon, WA

360-424-0800
Reservations Available

www.eaglemontgolf.com

Eaglemont has outstanding views of Mt. Baker and the Skagit Valley, plus it's a tough little course that will test your accuracy. Rolling fairways, mature trees, white sand and water provide plenty of challenge. The course rating is 74.8, the slope 149 and there are 5 sets of tees; from the forward tees the total distance is 5140 yards.

All green fees include a golf cart; they are required at Eaglemont. Friday thru Sunday as well as all major holidays 9 holes will cost you $30 and 18 for $62, or you can play all day for $77. The rest of the week you'll pay $30, $52 and $67.

Early bird rates are good until 9:00 am when 18 holes will cost you $42 Monday thru Thursday and $52 Friday thru Sunday. Twilight rates start at 2:00 pm. For 18 holes the rate is $40 early in the week and $52 Friday thru Sunday. Seniors age 60 and older can play 18 holes on weekdays for $42.

Winter rates are $25-28 for 9 holes, $42-47 for 18, and $57-62 to play all day. The lower amounts are for Monday thru Thursday, the higher sums Friday thru Sunday.

Facilities include a new clubhouse, a driving range, restaurant and lounge with banquet facilities, fitness center and a full-service pro shop.

Ask at the pro shop for help with tournament planning. They can also set you up with private or group lessons.

Directions: Located 3 miles west of downtown Mt. Vernon. Follow East Division Street for 2.1 miles, turn right onto S. Waugh Road and after .8 mile turn left onto the golf course road.

Overlook Golf Course

9 Holes ◇ Par 33 ◇ Length 2213 yards ◇ $-$$

17523 State Highway 9 ◇ Mt. Vernon, WA

360-422-6444 ◇ Reservations Available

www.overlookgc.com

This challenging course has a great view of Big Lake and the surrounding mountains. Designed by Neil Hansen and opened in 1985, the terrain has some hills and a little water. The slope is 97 and the course rating 60.2. A canal brings water into play on 5 holes.

You can play Overlook year round weather permitting. The total distance from the forward tees is 1809 yards.

Weekday green fees are $16 for 9 holes or $25 for 18. On weekends and holidays you'll pay $18 or $29. Monday thru Friday seniors can play for $16 and $23 and juniors pay $10 and $18.

They don't rent golf clubs but pull carts are $3 and motorized carts $15 for 9 holes and $26 for 18.

Facilities include a putting and chipping area, a pro shop where you can get help with tournament planning and arrange for lessons, plus a snack bar where you can get a cold beer.

They have a TruGolf golf simulator where you can have your swing analyzed, balls are $8.

Directions: Located southeast of town. Follow East Division for 3.6 miles, turn right onto Highway 9 and follow this south 2.4 miles to the golf course.

North Bend

Cascade Golf Course

9 Holes ◇ Par 36 ◇ Length 2691 yards ◇ $-$$

14319 436th Avenue SE ◇ North Bend, WA

425-888-4653 ◇ Reservations Available

www.cascadegolfcourse.com

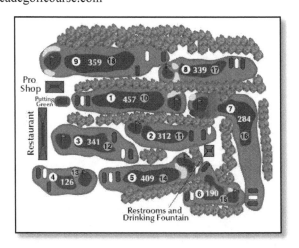

The Cascade Golf Course is surrounded by gorgeous snow-capped mountains. Built in 1950, the terrain is flat and easy to walk. Evergreens divide the fairways; the slope is 93 and the course rating 62.8. This course has one pond, some sand, a visiting elk herd, and is one of the driest courses in this area. The 7th hole is challenging with a dogleg and a pond; from the forward tees the total 9-hole distance is 2458 yards.

Green fees are cheapest in the winter when 9 holes will cost you $15 and 18 holes $22 all week long. Juniors play for $11 and $16, those under 7 are free and seniors play for $14 and $21. In the spring the junior and under 7 rate is the same but the general public pays $16 and $25, and seniors $14 and $22. Summer fees are $18 and $27 for everyone and $2 cheaper for seniors.

You can rent golf clubs for $7 and $10, pull carts are $3.50 and $5, motorized carts $16 and $26. The trail fee to bring your own cart is $3.50 for 9 holes or $5 if playing 18.

Facilities include a putting green, full-service pro shop, an interesting general store and the Riverbend Cafe where you can get a hot meal and a cold beer. At the pro shop you can get help with tournament planning and sign up for lessons.

Directions: Located just off I-90 via exit #32, marked 436th Avenue, turn right and look to the right; the café and golf course are right there, just past 142nd Street.

North Bonneville

Beacon Rock Golf Course

9 Holes ◇ Par 36 ◇ Length 2797 yards ◇ $-$$

102 Grenia Road ◇ North Bonneville, WA

509-427-5730 ◇ Reservations Available

www.beaconrockgolf.com

This course is located in the beautiful Columbia River Gorge and offers outstanding views of Beacon Rock and snow-covered mountains. A flat course, it opened in 1971. The slope is 115 and the course rating 69.7. The distance from the women's tees is 2540 yards. You'll find plenty of trees plus water on nearly every hole.

On weekends and holidays you'll pay $17 for 9 holes or $29 for 18. The rest of the week it will cost you $15 or $26. Twilight rates begin at 4:00 pm when 18 holes drop to $22 on weekends and holidays, $20 on weekdays.

Winter rates are in effect November thru February when everyone pays $1 per hole. In March it's $11 for 9 holes or $20 for 18, add $1 for weekend play. Pull carts rent for $2.50 and $4, and motorized carts $14 and $24. The trail fee when you bring your own cart is $3 for 9 holes or $5 for 18.

Facilities include a restaurant where beer is served and a putting green.

Directions: Located along Highway 14, 2 miles east of Beacon Rock State Park.

Olympia

Capitol City Golf Course
18 Holes ◇ Par 72 ◇ Length 6578 yards ◇ $-$$
5225 Yelm Highway SE ◇ Olympia, WA
360-491-5111 ◇ Reservations Available
www.golfcapitolcity.com

This year-round course has a great view of Mt. Rainier and is one of the most playable winter courses in the Pacific Northwest. Capital City is flat to mildly rolling and kept in excellent condition. You'll encounter narrow tree-lined fairways, plenty of sand and large greens. Built in 1962, the total distance from the forward tees is 5993 yards. The course rating is 70.9 and the slope 124.

Green fees Friday thru Sunday are $20 for 9 holes or $32 for 18. The rest of the week you'll pay $15 and $25. Active military and seniors play 18 holes on weekends for $29 and during the week for $23. Juniors pay $16 all week long.

The Twilight Rate begins at 2:00 pm and is $18 on weekdays or $29 on weekends and holidays. A Super Twilight Rate begins at 4:00 pm and is $13.80 seven days a week.

Golf clubs rent for $25 and $35, pull carts $4 and motorized carts $9 and $14.50 per rider. Facilities include a restaurant and lounge, full-service pro shop and driving range.

Golf lessons and help with tournament planning are available at the pro shop. At the driving range you'll pay $4.50 to $8 for a bucket of balls.

Directions: To find this course leave I-5 at exit #109, follow College Street to Yelm Highway and turn left. The course is 6 blocks.

Delphi Golf Course

9 Holes ◇ Par 32 ◇ Length 1937 yards ◇ $

6340 Neylon Drive SW ◇ Olympia, WA

360-357-6437 ◇ Reservations Available

www.delphigolfcourse.com

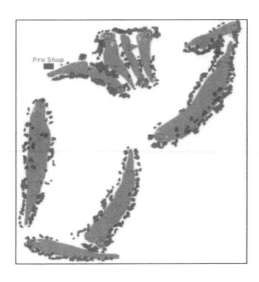

The Delphi course requires a good deal of accuracy with its small, undulating greens. Built in 1973, it was designed by Glen Correa and has three sets of tees. The terrain is mostly flat and the greens are bordered by trees. Sand and water come into play throughout the game. The 5th hole is played over water for par 3. The course rating is 60.6 and the slope 102. From the women's tees par is 34 and the total distance is 1789 yards.

On weekends you'll pay $16 for 9 holes or $22 for 18. Weekdays you pay $14 and $20. Seniors, active military members and juniors can play 9 holes Monday thru Friday for $11 or 18 for $16.

Pull carts rent for $3, motorized carts are $11 and $18, and if you bring your own cart the trail fee is $5.

They have a snack bar where you can get snacks and cold beer, and a pro shop. Lessons and help with tournament planning are available at the pro shop.

Directions: Located southwest of town. Follow Highway 101 North toward Aberdeen and take the Black Lake exit; turn left and go 3.6 miles, follow 62nd Avenue SW .7 mile and take a slight left onto Delphi Road SW.

Scott Lake Golf Course
9 Holes <> Par 35
Length 2547 yards <> $

11746 Scott Creek Drive SW
Olympia, WA

360-352-4838
Reservations Available

The Scott Lake course has lots of water hazards, fantastic greens and a terrain that is flat and easy to walk. Built in 1964 a creek cuts through the fairways and deer and geese are often spotted.

The course rating is 31.2 and the slope 94. From the women's tees the total distance is 2131 yards and par is 36.

Weekday green fees are $11 for 9 holes or $18 for 18. On weekends and holidays you'll pay $12 or $20. Juniors and seniors can play on weekdays for $9 and $15. Golf clubs rent for $4 and $6, pull carts are a flat $3 and motorized carts are $11 for 9 holes or $20 for 18.

Facilities include a chipping green, practice bunker, a restaurant that serves beer and wine and a pro shop.

Directions: Leave I-5 at exit #99 for Case Road, turn right and follow this to Scott Lake; you'll find signs to direct you from there.

Orting

High Cedars Golf Club

27 Holes ◇ Par 72 ◇ Length 6647 yards ◇ $-$$$

14604 149th Street Court E ◇ Orting, WA

360-893-3171 ◇ Reservations Available

www.highcedars.com

High Cedars has a great view of Mt. Rainier and offers both a championship 18-hole course and an executive 9-hole course. The championship course winds through old growth maple and cedar trees, and around natural hazards formed by the Puyallup River.

The course rating is 71.1 and the slope 119. From the forward tees the total distance is 5295 yards. The executive course is 1518 yards from the back tees with a slope of 87 and a course rating of 56.2. From the forward tees the total distance is 1210 yards.

Green fees on the 18-hole championship course Monday thru Thursday are $16 for 9 holes or $38 for 18. The rest of the week you'll pay $48 for 18 holes. On the executive course 18 holes are $16 on weekdays and $18 on weekends; 9 holes are $12 and $14. The senior special is $14 and $24 and juniors play for $10. Clubs rent for $14 and $20, and motorized carts are $10 and $14 per rider.

You'll find a putting green, chipping area, and a coffee shop serving cold beer, plus a full-service pro shop and driving range with lots of covered stalls.

At the pro shop you can get help with tournament planning. They also offer private and group lessons. At the driving range you'll find both grass and mat tees and range balls are $7 for a large bucket.

Directions: To reach the course take Highway 162 north of Orting 1 mile.

Port Ludlow

Resort at Port Ludlow Golf Course

27 Holes ◇ Par 36 ◇ Length 3340 yards ◇ $$-$$$

751 Highland Drive ◇ Port Ludlow, WA

360-437-0272 ◇ Reservations Available

www.portludlowresort.com

THE RESORT AT PORT LUDLOW

HOLE	1	2	3	4	5	6	7	8	9	OUT		10	11	12	13	14	15	16	17	18	IN	TOT 18
Black Tees	424	342	178	490	397	143	412	590/564	381	3357	N I T I A L	366	398	539	428	253	428	409	206/173	497/467	3504	6861
Blue Tees	379	322	162	465	364	128	384	515	367	3086		347	392	513	396	219	381	370	161	452	3231	6317
White Tees	355	294	156	434	353/322	107	363	486	337/330	2879		329	383	493	350	208/201	362	349	156	433	3063	5942
Handicap	9	13	15	1	3	17	11	5	7			12	10	4	2	16	8	14	18	6		
Par	4	4	3	5	4	3	4	5	4	36		4	4	5	4	3	4	4	3	5	36	72
Handicap	11	13	15	1	9	17	7	3	5			14	10	2	6	16	8	12	18	4		
Gold Tees	284	279	144	385	252	90	345	405	300	2484		296	323	445	267	177/138	319	306	146/128	402/380	2681	5165
Scorer:											Attest:								Date:			

Designed by Robert Muir Graves this course first opened in 1975; in 1993 they added their third nine. The terrain is very hilly and it has tree-lined fairways, elevated tees and plenty of sand. Surrounded by a forest, it also has a number of creeks and ponds, making it a pretty challenging course.

The 3397 yard **Tide Course** has lots of water, a creek and numerous ponds and some interesting elevation changes.

On the 3340 yard **Timber Course** you'll encounter some water, lots of trees, a couple of doglegs and some good downhill shots.

The 3326 yard **Trail Course** has numerous small ponds and is quite scenic; this course is currently closed but will open again shortly.

Each course has a par of 36. The slope is 124 and course rating 70.3.

Green fees June thru September are $55 Monday thru Thursday and $60 Friday thru Sunday as well as all holidays. October thru December you'll pay $30 and $35. Motorized carts rent for $10 per person when playing 9 holes and $15 each for 18 holes.

Port Ludlow Resort offers vacation accommodations, a marina, restaurant and lounge, full-service pro shop, snack bar and driving range. At the pro shop you can get help with tournament planning and set up lessons.

Directions: Located just west of the Hood Canal Bridge. From downtown Port Ludlow take Oak Bay Road .8 mile to Walker Way, turn left on Paradise Bay Road and follow this for 1.5 miles to Teal Lake Road. Turn right and immediately take the first right onto Highland Drive.

Port Orchard

Horseshoe Lake Golf Course

18 Holes ◇ Par 71 ◇ Length 6005 yards ◇ $$

1250 SW Clubhouse Court ◇ Port Orchard, WA

253-857-3326 ◇ Reservations Available

www.hlgolf.com

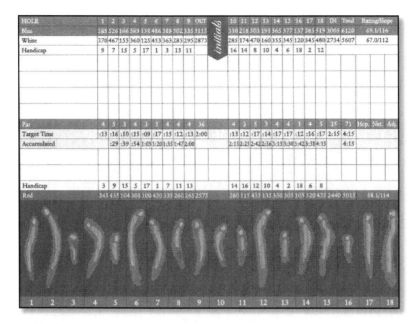

HOLE	1	2	3	4	5	6	7	8	9	OUT		10	11	12	13	14	15	16	17	18	IN	Total	Rating/Slope
Blue	385	526	166	389	138	486	388	302	335	3115		310	218	303	191	365	377	137	385	519	3005	6120	69.1/116
White	370	467	155	360	125	453	363	285	295	2873		285	174	470	160	355	345	120	345	480	2734	5607	67.0/112
Handicap	9	7	15	5	17	1	3	13	11			16	14	8	10	4	6	18	2	12			
Par	4	5	3	4	3	5	4	4	4	36		4	3	5	3	4	4	3	4	5	35	71	Hcp. Net. Adj.
Target Time	:13	:16	:10	:15	:09	:17	:15	:12	:13	2:00		:13	:12	:17	:14	:17	:17	:12	:16	:17	2:15	4:15	
Accumulated	:29	:39	:54	1:03	1:20	1:35	1:47	2:00				2:13	2:25	2:42	2:56	3:13	3:30	3:42	3:58	4:15		4:15	
Handicap	3	9	15	5	17	1	7	11	13			14	16	12	10	4	2	18	6	8			
Red	345	435	104	301	100	430	335	260	265	2575		260	115	435	135	330	305	105	320	435	2440	5015	68.1/114

You'll find a terrific view of the Olympic Mountains at Horseshoe Lake. Designed by Jim Richardson, the course was completed in 1992 and is open year round. The slope is 115 and the rating 68.

You'll find easy-to-walk sculpted fairways on the front nine along with three lakes and lots of evergreens. The back nine is hilly and crosses the canyon twice. From the women's tees the total distance is 5035 yards.

Friday thru Sunday you'll pay $25 for 9 holes or with a motorized cart $35 for 9 holes or $49 for 18. Monday thru Thursday it's $25 to walk 9 holes and with a cart $35 for 9 or $55 for 18 holes.

Twilight starts at 2:00 pm when the rate with a cart drops to $40 for 18 holes all week long. Juniors play for $20 all week long and seniors pay $47 for 18 holes with a cart. All day add-ons are just $20.

Facilities include a restaurant/lounge with a banquet area, full-service pro shop, driving range and snack bar. Lessons and help with tournament planning are available.

Directions: Located south of town. Take Highway 160/166 to Port Orchard Blvd. and follow this for 1.1 miles, turn right on Tremont St. W and after .9 mile take a left on Pottery Avenue. After .9 mile this road becomes Sidney Road SW. Follow this another 7.7 miles, the course will be on the right.

McCormick Woods Golf Course

18 Holes ◇ Par 72 ◇ Length 7040 yards ◇ $-$$$

5155 McCormick Woods Drive SW ◇ Port Orchard, WA

360-895-0130 ◇ Reservations Available

www.mccormickwoodsgolf.com

This year-round course was built in 1986 and carved out of an area of old-growth timber. Designed by Jack Frei, the front nine is fairly flat but the back nine has rolling hills with some elevated holes. Each hole has five separate tees offering all levels of golfers a terrific challenge.

Water comes into play on 8 holes, sand on 14 and the fairways are tree lined and well separated. The slope is 134 and the rating 74.3. The forward tees have a distance of 5299 yards.

You'll find a terrific view of Mt. Rainier and might even spot some wildlife on this course.

Green fees Monday thru Thursday are $29 for 9 holes and $49 for 18. On Fridays it's $29 and $54 and on weekends $39 and $64. Seniors receive 10% off Monday thru Friday and active military members 20%. Twilight begins at 3:30 pm and is $17 or $29. Juniors play for $10 and $15.

Push carts are $8 and power carts $15 per rider. You'll find a pro shop, snack bar, chipping and putting greens, practice bunkers and a driving range. Lessons are available.

Directions: Located southwest of downtown Port Orchard. Take Highway 160/166 to Port Orchard Blvd., follow this 1.1 miles and turn right on Tremont Street W. After .7 mile take Old Clifton Road for 2 miles and turn left onto McCormick Woods Drive SW.

Trophy Lake Golf Course

18 Holes ◇ Par 72 ◇ Length 7206 yards ◇ $$$

3900 SW Lake Flora Road ◇ Port Orchard, WA

360-874-8337 ◇ Reservations Available

www.trophylakegolf.com

This spot offers a unique northwest combination, fishing and golf. Designed by John Fought, it has lots of sand, water and trees. The quiet setting offers gorgeous views of Mt. Rainier and the Olympic Mountains. Two of the course ponds are stocked with rainbow trout. They have a strict dress code; no denim is allowed on the course.

Green fees Friday thru Sunday and on all major holidays are $75 for 18 holes. Come after 2:00 pm and you'll pay $59. After 5:00 pm it's $42. Monday thru Thursday green fees are $50 if you play before 8:00 am, $60 during prime time, $50 after 3:00 pm and $35 after 5:00 pm.

Facilities include a lodge-style clubhouse, practice putting and chipping areas, a full-service pro shop and a driving range. On the driving range you'll pay $5 for a small bucket of balls or $8 for a large one. The Dry Fly Cafe, overlooking the 18th green, has a full bar and serves home-style food.

Directions: Located south of downtown Port Orchard. Take Highway 160 west and turn right onto SW Sedgwick Road. This becomes Glenwood Road SW and then SW Lake Flora Road. The course is on the left.

Village Greens Golf Club

18 Holes ◇ Par 58 ◇ Length 3255 yards ◇ $

2298 Fircrest Drive SE ◇ Port Orchard, WA

360-871-1222

www.kitsapgov.com/parks/Parks/Pages/villagegreensgolfcourse.htm

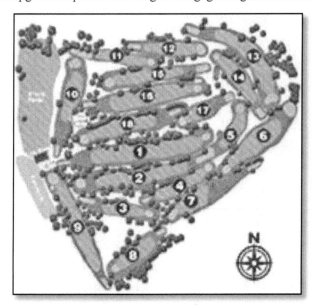

This Kitsap County course is kept in excellent condition and open every day but Christmas, from daylight to dark. It first opened in 1958, has a rolling terrain that stays dry throughout the winter and provides a great view of Mt. Rainier.

Tall trees, raised greens, water on 11 out of 18 holes and rocks add challenge. The slope is 87 and rating 57.7. Two sets of tees are available.

You can play all day for $16.50 so bring lunch! Seniors and military personnel including dependents of active military members can play for $13.20. Juniors age 5-18 pay $11. Clubs rent for $12, $8 to juniors, and pull carts are $3.26. Motorized carts are not available.

Golf lessons and help with tournament planning are available at the pro shop. They have a practice area and a covered, lighted driving range where you can get a medium bucket of balls for $5.50 or a large one for $8.75.

Directions: Take the second Port Orchard exit off Highway 16 and follow this road past 4 stop lights. At the stop sign, Fircrest Drive, turn right.

Port Townsend

Discovery Bay Golf Club
18 Holes ◇ Par 72 ◇ Length 6641 yards ◇ $$-$$$
7401 Cape George Road ◇ Port Townsend, WA
360-385-0704
www.discoverybaygolfcourse.com

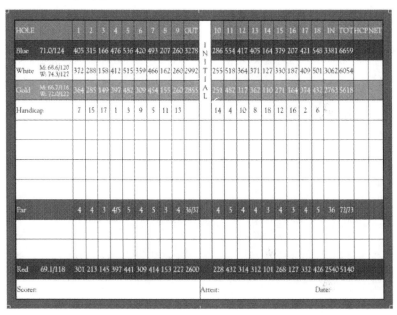

HOLE	1	2	3	4	5	6	7	8	9	OUT		10	11	12	13	14	15	16	17	18	IN	TOT	HCP	NET
Blue 71.0/124	405	315	166	476	536	420	493	207	260	3278		286	554	417	405	164	379	207	421	548	3381	6659		
White M: 68.6/120 W: 74.3/127	372	288	158	412	515	359	466	162	260	2992		255	518	364	371	127	330	187	409	501	3062	6054		
Gold M: 66.7/116 W: 72.0/122	364	285	149	397	482	309	454	155	260	2855		251	482	117	362	110	271	164	374	432	2763	5618		
Handicap	7	15	17	1	3	9	5	11	13			14	4	10	8	18	12	16	2	6				
Par	4	4	3	4/5	5	4	5	3	4	36/37		4	5	4	4	3	4	3	4	5	36	72/73		
Red 69.1/118	301	213	145	397	441	309	414	153	227	2600		228	432	314	312	101	268	127	332	426	2540	5140		

Scorer: Attest: Date:

This course has a great view of Discovery Bay and the Olympic Mountains, two 9-hole golf courses and fairways surrounded by huge trees. Formerly called Chevy Chase Golf Course, and a year-round course, it was constructed in 1925. Early morning golfers quite often spot deer and rabbits on the fairways.

The back nine, **Forest Course**, opened in 1997. **Farm Course** is the front nine. Discover Bay's terrain is relatively flat, has a slope of 124 and a rating of 71. Three sets of tees are available. From the forward tees the total distance is 5170 yards.

Green fees weekends and holidays are $27 for 9 holes or $45 for 18. Seniors 60 and older play for $22 and $35 and juniors under 18 play for $7 and $12. Weekday rates are $23 and $38. Seniors pay $18 and $29 and juniors $7 and $12. Twilight rates are $20 and $29. Add $6 for a motorized cart.

Golf clubs rent for $12 and $20, pull carts $4 and $6 and motorized carts $12 and $18 for a single player.

They have a snack bar with beer and wine, banquet facilities, a full-service pro shop and a driving range. At the pro shop you can sign up for lessons and get help with tournament planning.

The driving range has mat tees. A small bucket of balls is $4 and a large $6.

Directions: Head south on Highway 20 and at the edge of town stay right on Discovery Road, travel 5 miles and turn right in front of the tennis court.

Port Townsend Golf Club

9 Holes ◇ Par 35 ◇ Length 2800 yards ◇ $-$$

1948 Blaine Street ◇ Port Townsend, WA

360-385-4547 ◇ Reservations Available

www.porttownsendgolf.com

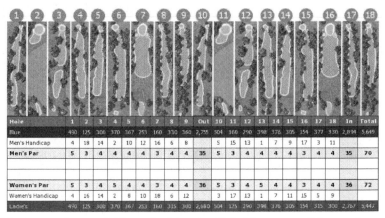

Hole	1	2	3	4	5	6	7	8	9	Out	10	11	12	13	14	15	16	17	18	In	Total
Blue	490	125	300	370	367	253	160	330	360	2,755	504	160	290	398	376	305	154	377	330	2,894	5,649
Men's Handicap	4	18	14	2	10	12	16	6	8		5	15	13	1	7	9	17	3	11		
Men's Par	5	3	4	4	4	4	3	4	4	35	5	3	4	4	4	4	3	4	4	35	70
Women's Par	5	3	4	5	4	4	3	4	4	36	5	3	4	5	4	4	3	4	4	36	72
Women's Handicap	4	16	14	2	8	10	18	6	12		3	17	13	1	7	11	15	5	9		
Ladie's	490	125	300	370	367	253	160	315	300	2,680	504	125	290	398	376	305	154	315	300	2,767	5,447

This course sits on a hill overlooking the Kaitai Lagoon and has a view of Port Townsend Bay as well as the Olympic Mountains. The layout is short, the fairways wide and the greens small.

Built in 1925, and open year round, the course rating is 32.9 and the slope 114. In the fall when the seasons change this is a real pretty course. Water can be a problem in the winter.

Green fees are $16.50 for 9 holes or $25 for 18. In the winter they drop as low as $14 and $19. Seniors can play weekdays for $14 and $19 and they only need be 55 or older. Juniors play for $7 and $10.

They offer a Working Person Special on weekdays after 3:00 pm when anyone can play 9 holes for $14 or 18 for $19.

Golf clubs rent for $8 and $13, pull carts are $2 and $3 and motorized carts are $8.50 per rider on 9 holes or $12.50 on 18.

They have a restaurant and lounge with a banquet area, a full-service pro shop and an 18-tee driving range.

A bucket of balls on the driving range will cost you $3.50 for a small bucket, $6 for medium or $10 for a large bucket. Lessons and help with tournament planning are available at the pro shop.

Directions: Located right in town, where Blaine Street meets the Lagoon.

Randle

Maple Grove Golf Course

9 Holes ◇ Par 31 ◇ Length 1521 yards ◇ $

175 Highway 131 ◇ Randle, WA

360-497-2741

Maple Grove opened in 1987, and is part of the 175-site Maple Grove RV Resort. The terrain is flat to slightly hilly, but easy to walk, with some water hazards and sand traps.

It has a nice view of the Cascade Mountains and is open year round. The slope is 79 and the course rating 28.2; from the forward tees the total distance is 1422 yards.

You can play all day at Maple Grove for $19 or you can pay $10 for 9 holes and $14 for 18. Golf clubs rent for $3 per 9 holes and push carts are $2.

They do not have motorized carts for rent but you can bring your own.

Facilities include a restaurant with beer and wine, a pro shop and RV park.

Directions: Located on the south side of Highway 12.

Ridgefield

Tri Mountain Golf Course

18 Holes ◇ Par 72

Length 6589 yards ◇ $$-$$$

1701 NW 299th Street
Ridgefield, WA

360-887-3004

Reservations Available

www.trimountaingolf.com

Built in 1994, Tri Mountain was designed by William G. Robinson. The view includes Mount St. Helens, Mt. Adams and Mt. Hood. Open year round, this course has rolling hills, 11 lakes and more than 60 bunkers.

Water comes into play on 12 holes and there are four sets of tees. The course rating is 72.5 and the slope 130; from the forward tees the distance is 5284 yards.

Friday thru Sunday and on holidays you'll pay $30 for 9 holes or $48 to play 18; Monday thru Thursday it will cost you $22 and $38. Juniors can play seven days a week for $10 and $14. Discount cards are available for seniors.

Golf clubs rent for $10-15 per 9 holes, depending on the quality you want. Everyone can take advantage of the $28 early bird rate Monday thru Thursday. Twilight rates are $28 Monday thru Thursday and $30 the rest of the week.

Pull carts are $4 and $6, and motorized carts rent for $10 and $16.

Facilities include a snack bar that serves cold beer and wine, plus a full-service pro shop and driving range. Lessons and help with tournament planning are available at the pro shop.

At the driving range you can get a bucket of balls for $4-6.

Directions: Leave I-5 North at exit #14 and turn right onto 269th Street; go to 11th Avenue and turn left and when you get to 299th Street turn left again. This leads to the course.

Seattle Area
(Seattle)

Green Lake Golf Course

9 Holes ◇ Par 27
Length 705 yards ◇ $

5701 Greenlake Way N
Seattle, WA

206-632-2280

The Green Lake Golf Course first opened in 1948. It operates March thru October from 9:00 am to dusk.

This Seattle course is a quick little pitch n' putt. The course is short with a flat terrain. The rating is 34.6 and the slope 116.

Green Lake is a fun course to play with the family or for working on your short game. The longest hole is only 115 yards.

Green fees are $7 for the first 9 holes and $3.50 for additional rounds. Everyone older than 64 or younger than 18 gets $1 off a 9-hole game.

Facilities are minimal. Machines offer cold pop and snacks.

Directions: This course is 5 miles north of downtown Seattle, near the southern tip of Green Lake and just west of I-5. Follow Aurora Avenue north to Green Lake and the course.

Interbay Golf Course

9 Holes ◇ Par 28 ◇ Length 1327 yards ◇ $

2501 15th Avenue W ◇ Seattle, WA

206-285-2200 ◇ Reservations Available

www.premiergc.com/-interbay-golf-center

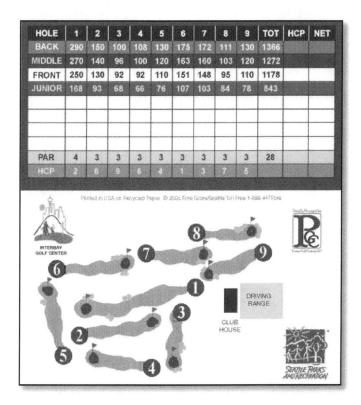

HOLE	1	2	3	4	5	6	7	8	9	TOT	HCP	NET
BACK	290	150	100	108	130	175	172	111	130	1366		
MIDDLE	270	140	96	100	120	163	160	103	120	1272		
FRONT	250	130	92	92	110	151	148	95	110	1178		
JUNIOR	168	93	68	68	76	107	103	84	78	843		
PAR	4	3	3	3	3	3	3	3	3	28		
HCP	2	6	9	8	4	1	3	7	5			

Interbay is open every day but Christmas and was designed by Jack Nicklaus. It first opened in 1997. It's a nice little inner-city course that can be played in under 1.5 hours.

Green fees Monday thru Friday are $15 for adults, $12 for seniors and $11 for junior golfers. On weekends the rates are $17 for everyone on the course. Pull carts rent for $4 and motorized carts $12 seven days a week.

Facilities include a snack bar with cold beer, putting and practice greens, a 2-story driving range and a full-service pro shop. Group and individual lessons are available. At the driving range you get 34 balls for $5, 68 for $8 and 102 will cost you $10.

Directions: Located less than 4 miles north of downtown; follow Elliott Avenue West along the water. Elliott Avenue becomes 15th Avenue; the course is .6 mile after the name change on the left.

Jackson Park Golf Course

27 Holes ◇ Par 71 ◇ Length 6247 yards ◇ $-$$

1000 NE 135th Street ◇ Seattle, WA

206-363-4747 ◇ Reservations Available

www.premiergc.com/-jackson-park-golf-course

Jackson Park first opened in 1930 and has both an 18-hole championship course and a 9-hole par three executive course. The championship course is always dry, fairly hilly and provides an interesting challenge.

The course rating is 67.4 and the slope 118. From the ladies' tees the total distance is 5413 yards for par 73. Built in 1930, Jackson Park is open every day but Christmas. The 9-hole course has a total distance of 1032 yards for a par 27.

Monday thru Friday on the 18-hole course adults pay $35; they pay $40 on weekends. On weekdays active military members, and seniors age 60 and to 75 can play 9 holes for $25. Seniors 75 and older as well as juniors pay just $15. Twilight rates begin 2 hours before closing when anyone can play for $16 seven days a week.

Green fees on the 9-hole course are $8.50 for 9 holes or $14 for 18 all week long. Juniors play for $6 and $10, and seniors for $7.50 and $12. Motorized carts are $17 and $26 and pull carts $4.

Facilities include a clubhouse, a restaurant where beer and wine are served, a driving range, full-service pro shop and snack bar. Lessons and help with tournament planning are available at the pro shop. Children under 8 are not allowed on either course. At the driving range you'll pay $5, $8 and $10 for a bucket of balls.

Directions: Located 9.5 miles north of downtown Seattle. Take I-5 north to exit #174, follow 5th Avenue to Roosevelt Way, go right to 10th Avenue and turn left. The course is .5 mile further, on the left.

Jefferson Park Golf Course

18 Holes ◇ Par 70 ◇ Length 6019 yards ◇ $$

4101 Beacon Avenue ◇ Seattle, WA

206-762-4513 ◇ Reservations Available

www.premiergc.com/-jefferson-park-golf-course

This Seattle course was built in 1928. Although the front nine is flat, the back nine is quite hilly. A challenging course, it is open year round and easy to walk. There are only a few sand traps and no water on this course. The total distance from the women's tees is 5524 yards for a par of 73.

Monday thru Friday adults pay $35 and $40 on weekends. On weekdays all active military members and seniors age 60 and to 75 can play 9 holes for $25. Seniors 75 and older as well as juniors pay just $15. Twilight begins 2 hours before closing when anyone can play for $16 seven days a week. Motorized carts are $17 and $26 on either course, pull carts are $4.

Facilities include a restaurant and lounge, driving range and full-service pro shop. They offer help with tournament planning and can set you up with lessons. At the driving range you'll pay $5, $8 or $10 for a bucket of balls.

Directions: Located 3.5 miles south of downtown via I-5. Take the Airport Way exit at the merge and leave I-5 on exit #163A. Go straight onto Columbian Way South. Turn left at S. Spokane Street and right onto Beacon Avenue. The course is .4 mile further.

West Seattle Golf Club

18 Holes ◇ Par 72 ◇ Length 6725 yards ◇ $-$$

4470 35th Avenue SW ◇ Seattle, WA

206-935-5187 ◇ Reservations Available

www.premiergc.com/-west-seattle-golf-course

Designed by H. Chandler Egan, the terrain on this course is slightly hilly. With a great view of downtown Seattle this course has been around since 1940. A creek runs past several holes and there are plenty of trees, several nice long shots and the greens are well bunkered. Open year round, the course rating is 71.7 and the slope 131. From the women's tees the total distance is 5535 yards.

Monday thru Friday it's $35 and $40 on weekends. On weekdays all active military members and seniors age 60 to 75 can play 9 holes for $28 and $40, and seniors 75 and older as well as juniors pay just $15. Twilight rates begin 2 hours before closing when anyone can play for $16 seven days a week. Motorized carts are $17 and $26 on either course and pull carts are $4.

They have a restaurant and lounge with banquet facilities plus a full-service pro shop. Lessons and help with tournament planning are available at the pro shop.

Directions: Located 5 miles south of downtown Seattle. Follow Highway 99S to the West Seattle Bridge exit and travel over the bridge. At 35th Avenue SW turn left and continue to the golf course.

(Bainbridge Island)

Meadowmeer Golf Club

9 Holes ◇ Par 72 ◇ Length 6502 yards ◇ $-$$

8530 NE Renny Lane ◇ Bainbridge Island, WA

206-842-2218 ◇ Reservations Needed

www.meadowmeergolf.com

This is a narrow, challenging course with well-placed bunkers, excellent greens, a rolling terrain and a great view of the Olympic Mountains. The slope is 117 and the course rating 67. Open dawn to dark, every day but Christmas, Meadowmeer is one of the most playable winter courses in the state. Built in 1972, the total distance from the women's tees is 2567 yards.

During the week you'll pay $20 for 9 holes or $25 for 18; on weekends it will cost you $25 and $30. On weekdays they have discounts for active military members, juniors and seniors. Motorized carts rent for $18 and $28.

Facilities include a snack bar where you can get cold beer and wine, banquet facilities and a full-service pro shop. Lessons and help with tournament planning can be arranged at the pro shop.

Directions: From the Seattle Ferry follow Highway 305 for 3.5 miles and then follow the signs to Meadowmeer.

(Bellevue)

Bellevue Golf Course

18 Holes ◇ Par 71 ◇ Length 6048 yards ◇ $$-$$$

5500 140th Avenue NE ◇ Bellevue, WA

425-452-7250 ◇ Reservations Needed

www.bellevuepgc.com

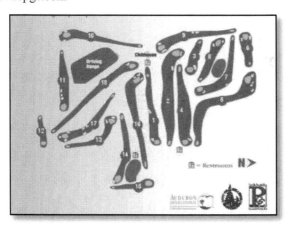

This course has a couple of ponds, plenty of trees, some interesting doglegs and holes that range in length from short par 3's to the par 5 long-driving 515 yard 18th hole. Open year round, the total distance from the women's tees is 4978 yards. The course rating is 68.4 and the slope 117.

Friday thru Sunday and on all major holidays green fees are $30 for 9 holes or $43 for 18. The rest of the week you'll pay $26 for 9 or $36 for 18.

Monday thru Thursday discounts are given to juniors and seniors; rates are $22 and $28. The rest of the week juniors and seniors can play here before 7:30 am for $25. Golf clubs rent for $15, pull carts $5 and motorized carts are $26 for two riders.

Facilities include the Bellevue Grill where you'll find hot food and cold beer, a driving range and pro shop. At the driving range you get 40 balls for $5, 80 for $9, 120 for $9 and 160 will cost $14. Help with tournament planning and lessons is available at the pro shop.

Directions: Leave I-405 north at the Redmond exit #18 and head east to 140th Avenue, turn right and go 1.5 miles to the course.

Crossroads Park Par 3 Golf Course

9 Holes ◇ Par 27
Length 837 yards ◇ $$
15801 NE 15th Street
Bellevue, WA
425-452-4873

www.bellevuepgc.com/-crossroads-par-3-course

Operated by the Bellevue Golf Club, Crossroads is open March thru October and provides a good little course for working on your irons. You'll find easy walking with some hills, grass tees and tree-lined fairways.

Most golfers play this entire course in about an hour; the holes range from 63-107 yards.

Green fees for 9 holes cost you $30 Friday thru Sunday and holidays and $26 the rest of the week. Juniors and seniors play for $22.

Clubs rent for $15, pull carts $5 and motorized carts are $26.

Facilities include a limited pro shop where you'll find snack machines and help with tournament planning as well as a driving range.

Directions: This course is behind the Crossroads Shopping Center. If you're driving north on 156th Avenue NE turn right onto 15th Street.

The Golf Club at Newcastle

36 Holes ◇ Par 72 ◇ Length 7024 yards ◇ $$$-$$$$

15500 Six Penny Lane ◇ Newcastle, WA

425-793-5566

www.newcastlegolf.com

Two 18-hole championship golf courses can be found at The Golf Club at Newcastle, along with stunning views of Lake Washington, Mt. Rainier and both the Olympic and Cascade Mountain ranges. They were designed by Robert Cupp.

The **Coal Creek** course (shown here) has a 621 yard opening hole. From the back tees the total distance is 7024 yards and from the forward tees 5153 yards. The course rating is 74.7 and the slope 147. This well-maintained course will test everyone's skills.

On the Coal Creek course green fees are the same seven days a week and include a motorized cart; peak rates are $165 but you can play for $110 between 1:00 pm and 3:00 pm and $100 from 3:00 pm to dusk. Undulating fairways, sharp drop-offs, tumbling water, hilly natural roughs and a view of the Seattle skyline await the Coal Creek golfer.

On the **China Creek** course the slope is 129 and the rating 72.3. From the back tees the distance is 6632 yards, it's 4782 yards from the forward tees. This course has tall trees, lots of natural areas, some well-placed bunkers, water, undulating fairways and a couple of interesting blind shots. The 18th hole has you shooting uphill, across a ravine and onto a sloping fairway.

At the China Creek course you'll pay $110 if you play before 1:00 pm, $85 between 1:00 pm and 3:00 pm, and $65 from 3:00 pm to closing every day of the week. Rates include a motorized cart.

They also have an 18-hole natural grass mini-course known as the Rusty Putter. Similar to the other courses in terrain, you'll find water, sand bunkers and a layout that's fun for adults as well as kids. Open weekends only from 6:30 am to 8:00 pm, adults pay $25 and kids younger than 18 play for $10 on this putting course.

Facilities include a 44,000-square-foot clubhouse, the elegant Calcutta Grill and Pub, the relaxing Wooly Toad lounge, year-round practice facilities and a full-service pro shop.

At the pro shop you can arrange for individual or group lessons and get help with tournament planning.

The practice facility has grass tees May thru September and is open from 8:00 am to dusk. Mat stations are used the balance of the year and they are open 6:30 am to 9:30 pm with the exception of Tuesdays when they open one hour later and Mondays when they close an hour early.

Directions: Located 7 miles south of Bellevue. Take I-405 toward Renton and follow the Coal Creek Parkway exit, #10 and after 2.8 miles turn left on SE 72nd/Newcastle Way and then left onto Newcastle Golf Club Road. After 1.6 miles turn right on 155th Avenue SE and take the first right onto Six Penny Lane. The course is .6 mile.

(Bothell)

White Horse Golf Club

18 Holes ◇ Par 72 ◇ Length 7093 yards ◇ $$-$$$

16721 96th Avenue NE ◇ Kingston, WA

360-297-4468 ◇ Reservations Available

www.whitehorsegolf.com

This course is not easy but it is fun; the greens are fast and accurate shots are needed on the fairways. The scenery is outstanding and the course well maintained. The back nine is a more forgiving than the front nine; no two holes play the same. The course rating is 74.9 and the slope 144. From the forward tees the total distance is 5022 yards. Four sets of tees are available.

Peak season green fees on weekends and holidays are $50-60 for 18 holes. Friday it's $29 for 9 holes and $53 for 18 and the rest of the week you can play for $25 and $45. Seniors play Monday thru Friday for $25 and $35, active military $35 and $45 and junior for $10. Motorized carts rent for $10 and $18 per rider.

Off-season green fees are $25 and $35 weekends and holidays and $20 or $29 weekdays. Seniors play weekdays for $24 and juniors for $10. Active military members pay $22 for 9 holes or $28 for 18. Carts rent for $10 and $12 per rider.

Facilities include an 11-acre practice facility with a double-ended driving range, putting and chipping greens and a practice sand trap plus a pro shop. They offer a free shuttle from the ferry landing with advance arrangements.

Directions: Located west of Bothell. Follow Highway 527/533 for 4 miles and take Ballinger Way NE/Highway 104 for 8.1 miles to the Edmonds-Kingston Ferry. When you get off the ferry take Highway 305 to the Agate Pass Bridge, turn right at the stop light just past the bridge and follow Indianola Road to South Kingston Road. Turn left. The course is 1 mile further on the left.

(Clinton)

Island Greens

9 Holes ◇ Par 27 ◇ Length 1312 yards ◇ $

3890 E French Road ◇ Clinton, WA

360-579-6042 ◇ Reservations Available

www.whidbeyislandgreens.com

Wildlife abounds on this challenging little par three; deer, heron and ducks are often sighted. The course was carved out of a farm and the design follows the natural terrain.

With more than 250 rhododendrons, Island Greens is a beautiful place to play April thru June when the flowers are in full bloom. Hazards include ponds, wetlands and huge evergreens. Three sets of tees are available. Open dawn to dusk, the total distance from the ladies' tees is 761 yards.

Green fees are a real bargain, $10 and $15 on weekends and $9 and $14 the rest of the week. An attendant is in the pro shop most weekends; the rest of the time fees are on the honor system so bring exact change.

When the pro shop is open golf club sets and pull carts rent for $2 each. Facilities include a clubhouse with a limited pro shop and a driving range.

Directions: Located west of Clinton on Whidbey Island. Head west on Highway 525 for 1.5 miles, turn left onto Campbell Road, after .6 mile turn left on Cultus Bay Road and follow this for 1.6 miles. Turn right onto French Road. The course is .4 mile further on the left.

(Kent)

Riverbend Golf Complex

27 Holes ◇ Par 72 ◇ Length 6701 yards ◇ $-$$

2019 W Meeker Street ◇ Kent, WA

253-854-3673 ◇ Reservations Available

www.riverbendgolfcomplex.com

Riverbend has both an 18-hole and a 9-hole course plus an outstanding view of Mt. Rainier. Covering 130 acres, hazards include three lakes, lot of trees, dozens of bunkers and a river. The Green River cuts right through this relatively flat course. It is dry in the winter and only closed on Christmas Day. The women's tees have a total distance of 5485 yards. The 9-hole par 3 course is 1174 yards long.

There's a miniature golf course for the kids too.

Prime time green fees on the 18-hole course are $20 for 9 holes or $32 for 18. On weekdays you'll pay $16 and $28. Active military members and seniors can play for $16 and $24 on weekdays and juniors pay $9 and $18. Twilight rates begin at 2:00 pm and are $22 on weekdays or $24 on weekends. Super twilight rates begin at 4:00 pm when everyone plays for $12 seven days a week.

Golf clubs rent for $20 and $30, push carts $4 and $6, and motorized carts $9 and $14 per person.

Directions: Leave I-5 at the Kent/Des Moines exit and head east to Meeker Street where you will turn left.

(Lynnwood)

Lynnwood Municipal Golf Course

18 Holes ◇ Par 65 ◇ Length 4741 yards ◇ $$

19100 44th Avenue W ◇ Lynnwood, WA

425-672-4653 ◇ Reservations Available

www.lynnwoodgc.com

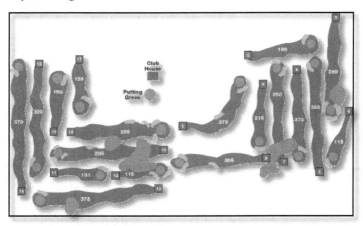

Lynnwood has tree-lined fairways with lots of sand bunkers and five ponds. Designed by John Steidel and opened in 1991 the terrain is flat and includes two sets of tees. The slope is 107 and the rating 62.9. From the forward tees the distance is 4094 yards. They are open dawn to dusk year round.

On weekends golfers pay $23 for 9 holes or $36 for 18; the weekday rate is $23 and $32. Monday thru Friday seniors age 62 and older pay $20 and $27. Juniors pay $10 and $15. College student with ID play during the week for $15 and $22. Golf clubs rent for $10-20, pull carts are $5 and motorized carts $8 per person for 9 holes, $14 each on 18.

Facilities include a putting green practice area, a restaurant, banquet room and pro shop. Lessons and help with tournament planning are available at the pro shop.

Directions: Located right in Lynnwood, behind Edmonds Community College. From the downtown area head east on 196th/Highway 524 for 1 mile and turn left onto 44th Avenue. The course is on the left.

(Mountlake Terrace)

Nile Shrine Golf Club

18 Holes ◇ Par 67 ◇ Length 5010 yards ◇ $-$$

6601 244th Street SW ◇ Mountlake Terrace, WA

425-774-9611 ◇ Reservations Available

www.nileshrine.org

Big evergreens, an easy-to-walk rolling terrain, doglegs, sand and water make this an interesting course. Some shots must be made over water others around corners or uphill. The course is pretty, the slope 107 and the rating 63.7. From the ladies' tees the total distance is 4503 yards.

Summer rates are in effect March thru October when you'll pay $26 and $36 on weekends and holidays, $19 and $29 during the week. Seniors rates for golfers age 65 and older are $17 and $26. Juniors play for the $15 and $25. During the Twilight Special adults play for $19 and $26. Motorized carts are $18 and $28, pull carts $4 and $6 and clubs rent for $10 and $15. Winter rates are $16 for 9 holes or $26 for 18 on weekends and holidays, $15 or $20 the rest of the week.

Facilities include a putting green, picnic area, a nice bar and grill and a full-service pro shop where you can get help with tournament planning and sign up for lessons.

Directions: Located southwest of town 1.5 miles; take the I-5 South ramp, merge onto 244th Street/Highway 204 and follow to course.

(Redmond)

The Golf Club at Redmond Ridge

18 Holes ◇ Par 70 ◇ Length 6503 yards ◇ $$$

11825 Trilogy Parkway NE ◇ Redmond, WA

425-836-1510 ◇ Reservations Available

www.redmondridgegolf.com

This course was designed by Gary Panks and is surrounded by tall trees. The terrain utilizes the landscapes natural water features and gentle hills. Views of the Cascade Mountains add to the beauty of this course. The course is well kept and sits in the Redmond watershed. It was formerly known as Trilogy Golf Club.

The course is open from 5:30 am to 7:00 pm. No denim is allowed on the course; a strict dress code is enforced.

Friday thru Sunday and on all major holidays you'll pay $95 for 18 holes; Monday thru Thursday its $85. There's a special beginning at 3:00 pm when you only pay $65 Friday thru Sunday and holidays or $60 Monday thru Thursday.

Facilities include a full-service pro shop, restaurant and lounge, driving range and banquet facilities. The Crooked Spoon Restaurant serves home-style food and cold beer and wine.

The driving range is open until 7:00 pm every day but Wednesday. They close at 5:00 pm on Wednesdays.

Directions: Located east of downtown Redmond. Take Avondale Road NE to NE Novelty Hill Road, and follow this for 3.5 miles. Turn left onto Trilogy Parkway NE. The course is on the left.

Willows Run Golf Club

45 Holes ◇ Par 72 ◇ Length 6803 yards ◇ $-$$$

10402 Willows Road NE ◇ Redmond, WA

425883-1200 ◇ Reservations Available

www.willowsrun.com

There are three golf courses at Willows Run. The **Coyote Creek** course (shown here) is 6344 yards from the back tees for par 72. From the forward tees the distance is 5441 yards.

The **Eagle's Talon** course encircles the Coyote Creek Course. The total distance is 6803 yards for par 72, from the forward tees the distance is 5763 yards. Both of these courses have lots of water.

The **Heron Links** course opened in 1999 and is a par 3 course. Holes range from 86-170 feet in length. They also have a miniature putting course, Rainbow Run.

May thru September on the 18-hole courses green fees are $60 Friday thru Sunday, $46 after noon and $36 after 3:00 pm. They have an Early Bird Special Fridays only for $41. Monday thru Thursday 18 holes will cost you $46; juniors, seniors and ladies can play for $31. Rates drop to $41 at noon and $36 after 3:00 pm.

Green fees on the 9-hole par 3 course Monday thru Thursday are $11; Friday thru Sunday you'll pay $13. Juniors age 13 and younger and seniors play for $9.

On the miniature course adults pay $9 and kids age 12 and younger $6. Come before 11:00 am and save $1 off regular rates.

Facilities include practice putting and chipping areas, a great restaurant, plus a driving range and full-service pro shop. Help with tournament planning and lessons are available at the pro shop.

Directions: Located north of downtown Redmond. Follow Redmond Way to Willows Road and turn right. After 1.5 miles you will see the course on the right hand side of the road.

(Renton)

Maplewood Golf Course

18 Holes ◇ Par 72 ◇ Length 6127 yards ◇ $$

4050 SE Maple Valley Hwy. ◇ Renton, WA

425-430-6800 ◇ Reservations Available

www.rentonwa.gov/maplewoodgolfcourse

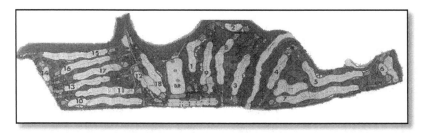

This course was built in 1927 and is open year round from sunrise until dark. The slope is 111 and the course rating 66. Three sets of tees are available. Water affects several holes, including the beautiful Cedar River which cuts between the 3rd and 4th fairways. This course operates as an Audubon Sanctuary and is run by the City of Renton. Mature trees, sand, doglegs and lakes will keep you on your toes.

April thru October green fees at Maplewood are $25 for 9 holes. 18 holes will cost you $34 on weekdays or $25 and $40 on weekends. Juniors can play 18 holes on weekdays for $18 and seniors for $25. In the summer motorized carts rent for $17 and $28.

November thru March green fees at Maplewood are $34 for 18 holes on weekends or $25 for 9 holes. The rest of the week you can play 9 or 18 holes for $25. Monday thru Friday seniors play for $17 and juniors $14. Winter rates for motorized carts are $14 per seat when playing 18 holes or $8.50 per seat for 9 holes.

You'll find a restaurant and lounge with banquet facilities, a full-service pro shop and a driving range. The 30-station driving range has mat tees. A bucket of balls is $2 for 20 balls.

Directions: Take exit #4 off I-405 and go east 2 miles.

(This is the end of the Seattle Area Listings)

Sedro Woolley

Gateway Golf Course

9 Holes ◇ Par 36 ◇ Length 3050 yards ◇ $-$$

1288 Fruitdale Road ◇ Sedro Woolley, WA

425-633-6547

www.gatewaygolfandrestaurant.com

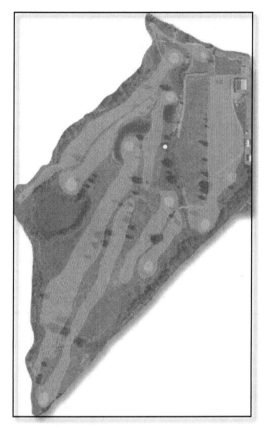

The terrain on this year-round course is a combination of flat and hilly and provides a nice view of the Cascade Mountains. The rating is 67.9 and the slope 115.

From the forward tees the distance is 2500 yards. Three tees are available to add variety to an 18-hole game. There are lots of roughs here, some on the fairways; houses overlook the fairways.

Green fees Friday thru Sunday and holidays is $18 for 9 or $29 for 18 and juniors pay $16 and $18. The rest of the week it's $16 and $25, seniors pay $14 and $23 and juniors $10 and $18.

Pull carts rent for $5 and motorized carts $15 and $26. Facilities include a new restaurant, putting and chipping greens, a practice range and a limited pro shop.

At the range a small bucket of balls is $5 and a large one $10.

Directions: Located 3 blocks off Highway 20.

Shelton

Lake Limerick Golf Club

9 Holes ◇ Par 36 ◇ Length 2898 yards ◇ $

E 790 St. Andrew Drive ◇ Shelton, WA

360-426-6290 ◇ Reservations Available

www.lakelimerick.com

Lake Limerick's narrow fairways are lined with trees and the terrain is fairly flat. Built in 1967, the slope is 120 and course rating 67.2 on this semi-private year-round golf course. Surrounded by fir trees Lake Limerick is a pretty course where golfers occasionally spot deer and raccoons. The terrain is fairly flat and easy to walk.

Spring and summer green fees are $20 for 9 holes or $29 for 18 on weekends or $18 and $27 during the week. Motorized carts are $15 for 9 holes or $25 for 18 and pull carts rent for $5. The trail fee when you bring your own cart is $6.

They have a restaurant/lounge, banquet facilities and a full-service pro shop. Tournament planning assistance and lessons are available at the pro shop.

Directions: Leave downtown heading north on Highway 3. At Mason Lake Road turn left and after 3 miles turn left again onto St. Andrew Drive.

Salish Cliffs Golf Club

18 Holes ◇ Par 72

Length 7269 yards ◇ $$-$$$

91 West State Route 108
Shelton, WA

360-462-3673
Reservations Available

www.salish-clifffs.com

Salish Cliffs Golf Club is part of the Little Creek Casino Resort and opened in 2011. The course rating is 75.4 and the slope 137 from the back tees. The total distance from the forward tees is 6312 yards.

There are lots of trees on this course and they separate the fairways well; doglegs, sand and water are also found on this course. Designed by Gene Bates, the course is surrounded by a lush forest. Strict dress code enforced.

Walking is not allowed on this course so all fees include a golf cart. They have a demand based pricing structure so the busier it is the more they charge. Green fees are about $99 Friday thru Sunday and holidays or $95 earlier in the week. Twilight rates begin at 3:00 pm when weekend rates become around $50, and Monday thru Thursday rates are $40.

Facilities include practice areas, a log clubhouse, restaurant and lounge, full-service pro shop and a driving range with grass tees. On the driving range you'll pay $5-10 for a bucket of balls. Help with tournament planning and lessons are available at the pro shop.

Directions: Located 6.5 miles south of downtown Shelton. Take Highway 3 to US 101 and follow this to Highway 108. The course is .4 mile on the left.

Snohomish

Echo Falls Country Club

18 Holes ◇ Par 70 ◇ Length 6189 yards ◇ $$-$$$

20414 121st Avenue SE ◇ Snohomish, WA

360-362-3000 ◇ Reservations Available

www.echofallsgolf.com

This country club is open year round and the 18th hole features an island green with a waterfall for a par three. Designed by Jack Frei, it first opened in 1992 and sports tree lined fairways, lots of bunkers and water hazards. It has great views of the Cascade and Olympic Mountains and four sets of tees per hole. The slope is 126 and the course rating of 68. From the women's tees the total distance is 4265 yards for par 71.

Green fees Friday thru Sunday and on all major holidays are $54 during peak season. The rest of the week you can play for $32. Twilight Specials are available only to members. They rent golf clubs for $50, pull carts are $6 and motorized carts $15 per seat.

Facilities include the Greenside Grill serving hot food and cold beer and wine, plus a banquet area, driving range and full-service pro shop. Help with tournament planning and lessons are available at the pro shop. At the driving range you can get a bucket of balls for $5-8.

Directions: Leave I-405 on Highway 522, go east 7 miles and turn right at the light onto Echo Lake Road. You can follow the course signs from there. The course is on the right side of the road.

Kenwanda Golf Course

18 Holes ◇ Par 69 ◇ Length 5336 yards ◇ $-$$

14030 Kenwanda Drive ◇ Snohomish, WA

360-668-1166 ◇ Reservations Available

www.kenwandagolf.com

Kenwanda is a flat year-round course with trees dividing the fairways. Built in 1962 this is a great winter course. The terrain has good slope, the greens are small and the fairways offer a wonderful view of the Snohomish Valley. Interconnecting fairways, doglegs, blind holes, mature trees, bunkers, water and plenty of slopes make this a challenging and fun course. From the ladies' tees par is 72.

On weekends you can play 9 holes for $20 or 18 holes for $30. On weekdays 9 holes are only $18. Twilight rates change so call ahead. Seniors and active military members save 10% off regular rates on non-holiday weekdays. Motorized carts are available and rent for $8 per seat when playing 9 holes or $12 for 18.

Facilities include a coffee shop where you can get cold beer and wine, plus a putting green and a full-service pro shop. Help with tournament planning is available at the pro shop.

Directions: Located 4 miles south of Snohomish, east of Highway 9. Take Broadway east .5 mile, turn left onto Connelly Street for .2 mile and turn left onto Kenwanda Drive.

Snohomish Public Golf Course

18 Holes ◇ Par 72 ◇ Length 6813 yards ◇ $-$$

7806 147th Avenue SE ◇ Snohomish, WA

360-568-2676 ◇ Reservations Available

www.snohomishgolfcourse.com

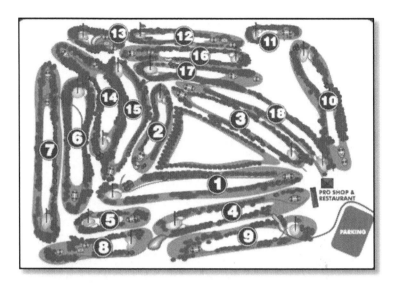

This Snohomish course has elevated greens, water hazards, rolling hills, tree lined fairways and lots of sand traps. It is long enough to challenge the good golfer but open enough for beginners. Three sets of tees are available. From the women's tees the total distance is 5325 yards for par 72. Open year round, the course rating is 72.3 and the slope 125.

Weekdays green fees are $19.50 for 9 holes or $31 for 18.On weekends and holidays it's $22 and $28. During the week they have an Early Bird Special of $25 for 18 holes that begins at 7:30 am. Juniors, seniors and active military play for $16.50 and $25.

All week long they have a Twilight special and it is $25 to play 18 holes during the week and $31 on weekends and holidays.

Golf clubs rent for $6-10, pull carts are $2 per 9 holes and motorized carts are $10-15 per rider The trail fee if you bring your own cart is $5.50.

They have a restaurant and lounge with banquet facilities, a full-service pro shop and driving range. At the driving range you can get a small bucket of balls for $3 or a large one for $5.

Lessons and help with tournament planning are available at the pro shop.

Directions: Located 3.6 miles west of downtown Snohomish. Follow 2nd Street until it becomes 92nd Street SE, take 88th Street for .7 mile, turn left onto 131st Avenue and take the first right onto 84th Avenue. Go left on 139th Avenue then right on 80th, left on 147th. Follow this road to the course. It is on the left.

Snoqualmie

Mt. Si Golf Course

18 Holes ⋄ Par 72 ⋄ Length 6261 yards ⋄ $$-$$$

9010 Boalch Avenue SE ⋄ Snoqualmie, WA

452-391-4926 ⋄ Reservations Available

www.mtsigolf.com

Mt. Si has both an 18-hole course and a little pitch and putt miniature course. This gently rolling course has some water and trees, is situated near the base of beautiful Mt. Si and offers lush green fairways. The slope is 117, the course rating 69.2 and three sets of tees are available. From the forward tees the total distance is 5475 yards. Open year round except Christmas. They operate from daylight to dusk.

On weekends and holidays you'll pay $29 for 9 holes or $49 for 18. Monday thru Wednesday the rates are $22 and $39 and if you come on Thursday or Friday you'll pay $25 and $43. Seniors and juniors can play 18 holes for $31 Monday thru Wednesday or $35 Thursday thru Friday. Golf clubs rent for $15 and $22, pull carts $3-5 and motorized carts $9-14 per rider. On the miniature course adults pay $6 and kids $4 for 9 holes.

You'll find a nice restaurant and lounge with banquet facilities, plus a driving range, snack bar and full-service pro shop. They can help you with tournament planning and lessons at the pro shop. At the driving range you'll find grass tees and pay $3 for 34 balls or $7 for 70.

Directions: Leave I-5 at exit #27, go 1 mile to the Snoqualmie Falls exit and follow the signs to Mt. Si Golf Course.

Stanwood

Kayak Point Golf Course

18 Holes ◇ Par 72 ◇ Length 6719 yards ◇ $$

15711 Marine Drive ◇ Stanwood, WA

360-652-9656 ◇ Reservations Available

www.golfkayak.com

The Kayak Point course was built in 1977, has a slope of 128 and a course rating of 72.2. You'll find thick woodlands separating the fairways, a sloping terrain, numerous bunkers and well-manicured greens on this challenging course. Views of Puget Sound and the Olympic Mountains, along with the opportunity to spot deer, raccoon or coyote, add to this course's attraction.

Designed by Ronald Fream, the total distance from the forward tees is 5332 yards. Open year round Kayak Point is a good winter course.

Green fees October thru March for 18 holes are $29 on weekdays and $40 on weekends and holidays. Twilight rates begin at 1:00 pm and everyone pays $22 and $24 seven days a week. Monday thru Friday seniors age 60 or older play for $15.

Motorized golf carts are $14 per person for 18 holes. On weekdays seniors pay $8 for a cart and the twilight cart rate is also $8.

Facilities include a driving range plus a restaurant and lounge with banquet facilities and a view of Puget Sound.

At the driving range you'll find grass tees and balls are $4 for 30 balls or $7 for 60. The full-service pro shop can provide help with tournament planning and set up lessons.

Directions: Located south of Stanwood. From I-5 North take exit #199 and turn left to follow Marine Drive for 13 miles.

Tacoma Area
(Tacoma)

Allenmore Public Golf Club

18 Holes ◇ Par 71 ◇ Length 6093 yards ◇ $$-$$$

2125 S Cedar ◇ Tacoma, WA

253-627-7211 ◇ Reservations Available

www.allenmoregolfcourse.com

The first nine holes at Allenmore were built around 1916 by Sam Allen; the second nine was added in 1935.

There is a large lake at its center, plus two smaller lakes on the 12th and 16th fairways. The course rating is 68.4 and the slope 115. Open year round, from 6:00 am to dusk, par from the women's tees is 74 for a total distance of 5652 yards.

This course offers Elk Club members reduced rates, as well as having public green fees.

On weekends public green fees are $28 for 9 holes or $44 for 18; the rest of the week you'll pay $27 or $40. Seniors can play Monday thru Friday for $17 and $24 and juniors pay $20 on weekdays or $25 on weekends.

Motorized carts are $10 per rider per 9 holes.

Facilities include a restaurant and lounge with banquet facilities, plus a driving range and full-service pro shop.

Directions: Leave I-5 at the Bremerton exit and follow Sprague Street to 19th, where you will turn left to the course.

Brookdale Golf Course

18 Holes ◇ Par 71 ◇ Length 6466 yards ◇ $-$$

1802 Brookdale Road E ◇ Tacoma, WA

253-537-4400 ◇ Reservations Available

www.brookdalegolfcourse.com

Built in 1931, Brookdale was designed by Christopher Mahan and is open year round. It offers an easy-to-walk terrain and is fun for all levels of golfers.

The slope is 117 and the course rating 70.1. From the ladies' tees par is 74 for a total distance of 5833 yards.

During the summer months you can get on the course at 6:00 am; the rest of the year you have to wait until 7:00 am. You'll find a gently rolling terrain, sand, doglegs, tall trees and a pleasant country-style course.

Green fees on Saturday and Sunday are $19 for 9 holes or $30 for 18. On weekdays you'll pay $17 or $25. Juniors can play Monday thru Friday for $10 and $15.

Golf clubs rent for $6 per 9 holes, pull carts are $4 and motorized carts $9 per rider for 9 holes or $12 for 18. If you bring your own cart the trail fee is $6.

Facilities include a restaurant and lounge, driving range and full-service pro shop. Lessons and help with tournament planning are available. The driving range has a 24-stall automatic warm-up center that is completely enclosed.

Directions: Leave I-5 on Highway 512, turn right toward Parkland and after about a mile turn left on 131st. The course is just a short distance from here.

Chambers Bay Golf Course

18 Holes ◇ Par 72 ◇ Length 7585 yards ◇ $$$$-$$$$$

6320 Grandview Drive W ◇ University Place, WA

253-460-4653 ◇ Reservations Available

www.chambersbaygolf.com

The views at Chambers Bay are awesome with Puget Sound and the islands in full view. Huge sand bunkers, rolling hills and tough shots make it an exciting course as well as scenic. Designed by Robert Trent Jones it opened in 2007 to rave reviews; the course rating is 76.8 and the slope 142. From the forward tees the total distance is 5253 yards.

You play in view of the sound on the first three holes then begin an uphill drive to the fourth hole; the 10th fairway is edged with 60' sand dunes and the 16th plays right along the water. Dress code enforced.

Peak season green fees June thru September include a cart and vary based on the time of day and day of the week. Washington residents pay around $215, seniors and active military members $169 and juniors age 14 to 17 who play with a paid adult $89. Off-season green fees are lower but vary too, it'll cost you around $175. Higher rates are charged Friday thru Sunday and on all major holidays.

Pull carts are included in your green fees. TaylorMade rental clubs are $55 and motorized carts are reserved for those with permanent disabilities. Using a golf cart makes a caddie mandatory.

Facilities include practice putting and chipping areas, a driving range, full-service pro shop and a restaurant and lounge with banquet facilities. You'll find help with tournament planning and lessons at the pro shop.

Directions: Located southwest of Tacoma. From I-5 South take exit #130 for South 56th Street. Keep to the right and take the Tacoma Mall ramp, turn left onto Tacoma Mall Blvd. and immediately turn right onto 56th Street West. Follow this for 2.1 miles, take Cirque Drive West for 3 miles, at the second round-about take the 2nd exit onto Grandview Drive West and drive .8 mile to the golf course.

Fort Steilacoom Golf Course

9 Holes ◇ Par 34 ◇ Length 2491 yards ◇ $-$$

8202 87th Avenue SW ◇ Tacoma, WA

253-588-0613 ◇ Reservations Available

www.lakespanawaygc.com/fort-steilacoom

Fort Steilacoom is a good course for beginners or those looking to tune up their game. The slope is 98 and the course rating 62.8. Two tees are found at each hole adding variety to an 18-hole game.

Open every day but Christmas, this course has been managed by Pierce County since 1971.

The terrain is flat and easy to walk, the fairways narrow and the greens small. The course rating is 62.1 and the slope 96. From the forward tees the total distance is 2379 yards.

Green fees are $17 for 9 holes or $22 for 18, seven days a week; seniors and college students can play for $12 or $17. Juniors play for $9 and $13.

Golf clubs rent for $15, pull carts $3 and $6 and motorized carts $15 for 9 holes or $22 for 18. If you bring your own cart the trail fee is $8.

Facilities include a restaurant and lounge, driving range and a full-service pro shop. Lessons and help with tournament planning are available. The driving range has a 24-stall automatic warm-up center that is completely enclosed.

Directions: Located southwest of downtown Tacoma. Take I-5 South to exit #129 the South 74th Street West ramp, turn right and 74th 2.3 miles until it becomes Custer Road West. Follow Custer 1.2 miles and take a slight right onto 88th Street SW, stay straight at Steilacoom Blvd. and after 1 mile turn right onto 87th Avenue SW. The course is .2 mile further on the left.

Highlands Golf Club

9 Holes ◇ Par 28 ◇ Length 1270 yards ◇ $

1400 Highland Parkway N ◇ Tacoma, WA

253-759-3622 ◇ Reservations Available

www.highlandsgolf.net

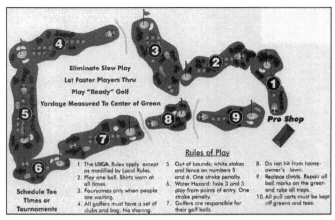

Tacoma's Highlands Golf & Racquet Club is nestled among the houses in the city's Westgate area. Opened in 1969, the course is level, includes two water holes and plenty of sand traps. You can play this course in less than 1.5 hours. It is open from 7:30 am to dusk every day but Christmas.

Green fees are $12 for 9 holes or $18 for 18 holes seven days a week. Seniors and juniors can play 9 holes for $10 or 18 for $16.

Facilities include a pro shop where you can get help with tournament planning and a clubhouse that is available for private tournaments.

Directions: Leave I-5 on Highway 16, take the 6th Avenue exit, turn right onto Westgate Boulevard, left on Highland Parkway North and left again after one block.

Meadow Park Golf Course

27 Holes ◇ Par 71 ◇ Length 6145 yards ◇ $-$$

7108 Lakewood Drive W ◇ Tacoma, WA

253-473-3033 ◇ Reservations Available

www.metroparkstacoma.org/meadow-park-golf-course

You'll find a sporty 9-hole as well as a challenging championship 18-hole course at Meadow Park. Both are fairly level with some hills and open year round. Three sets of tees are available and the distance from the forward tees on the 18-hole course is 5094 yards for par 73.

The slope is 118 and the course rating 69 on the 18-hole course. It is 76 and 56.8 on the 9-hole course. The shorter course has a total distance of 1600 yards for par 29. From the forward tees the distance is 1426 yards.

Off-season green fees on the 18-hole course Monday thru Friday are $25. On weekends and holidays they charge $30. Juniors pay $16 all week long. Adults pay $20 after 4:00 pm seven days a week.

On the 9-hole course adults pay $20 for 9 holes, seniors and active military $19 and juniors $16. Golf clubs rent for $10 and $14, pull carts are $5 and motorized carts are $10 and $15 per seat.

Amenities include putting and chipping greens, a restaurant and lounge with banquet facilities, a full-service pro shop and driving range. Lessons and help with tournament planning is available.

Directions: Take the 74th Street exit off I-5 at Tacoma. The course is just 1 block to the left.

North Shore Golf Club

18 Holes ◇ Par 71 ◇ Length 6305 yards ◇ $-$$

4101 North Shore Blvd. NE ◇ Tacoma, WA

253-927-1375 ◇ Reservations Available

www.northshoregc.net

North Shore is a dry winter course with a view of Mt. Rainier. Opened in 1961 it was designed by Al Smith. The front nine is fairly flat but the back nine has a couple of hills. It is well maintained with grass tees and large greens. Large evergreens divide the fairways. Open year round from dawn to dark the slope is 129 and the course rating 70.3.

Green fees are $19.21 for 9 holes or $31.44 for 18 on weekends and weekdays it's $13.97 or $24.45. Seniors can play Monday thru Friday for $20.80 for 18 holes and juniors pay $15 on weekdays and $18 on weekends. Active military members receive a 10% discount. Golf clubs rent for $13, pull carts are $3.50 and motorized carts are $10 per person for 18 holes.

You'll find a covered, lighted 65-tee driving range and teaching studio, chipping and putting greens, plus a well-stocked pro shop, a restaurant offering beer and wine and banquet facilities.

Directions: Leave I-5 at exit #142-B, go west 5 miles, turn left onto Nassau, go .5 mile, and follow the signs.

University Golf Club

9 Holes ◇ Par 35 ◇ Length 2732 yards ◇ $

754 124th Street S ◇ Tacoma, WA

253-535-7393

Hole	1	2	3	4	5	6	7	8	9	Out	Total
Mens	344	206	201	519	333	114	246	263	506	2,732	2,732
Men's Handicap	1	7	11	3	9	18	15	14	6		
Men's Par	4	3	3	5	4	3	4	4	5	35	35
Women's Par	4	4	3	5	4	3	4	4	5	36	36
Women's Handicap	1	7	11	3	9	18	15	14	6		
Ladies	344	206	201	519	333	114	246	263	506	2,732	2,732

Located on the Pacific Lutheran University campus and open year round, you can start at 6:30 am in the summer and 7:30 am in winter. It is flat and has great greens. The rating is 64.7 and the slope 101. This is dry winter course.

Green fees are $11 for 9 holes or $17 for 18 all week long. Monday thru Friday seniors and juniors play for $9 and $14. Current PLU students pay $5 and $8 all week long. Golf clubs rent for $5, pull carts $2, and motorized carts are $8 per 9 holes. If you bring your own cart the trail fee is $2-3.

Facilities include putting greens, a coffee shop and a full-service pro shop. Lessons and help with tournament planning are available at the pro shop.

Directions: Located 7 miles south of downtown Tacoma. Take exit #127 off I-5 and follow Highway 512 east about 2 miles to Pacific Avenue. Turn right and go to 125th Street. The course is at the corner of 125th and Yakima.

(Auburn)

Auburn Golf Club

18 Holes <> Par 71 <> Length 6014 yards <> $-$$

29630 Green River Road SE <> Auburn, WA

253-833-2350 <> Reservations Available

www.auburngolf.org

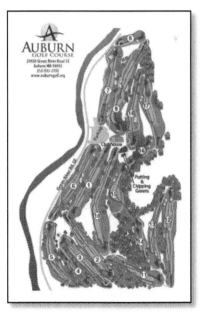

The Auburn Golf Club's front nine is flat, the back nine is hilly and water is found throughout the course. It opened in 1948 and hours are 8:00 am to sundown in the winter; in the summer they open at 7:00 am on weekdays and 5:00 am on weekends. The women's tees have a distance of 5571 yards. The rating is 69 and the slope 120. Hazards include a couple of ponds, blind shots, lots of mature trees and plenty of sand.

May thru September weekday green fees are $24 for 9 holes or $37 for 18. Seniors pay $18 and $30 and juniors $12 and $18. On weekends and holidays everyone pays $28 and $43. At twilight 18 holes will cost you $28.

Fall green fees are $16 and $28. On weekends and holidays you'll pay $20 or $31. Twilight rates begin at 1:30 pm and are $16 weekdays or $20 weekends and holidays. Seniors play 18 holes weekdays for $23, juniors for $14. Anyone who tees off before 8:30 am plays 9 for $14 or 18 for $20.

Clubs rent for $10 and $15, pull carts $4 and $6 and motorized carts $8 and $14 per seat. Bring your own cart and pay a trail fee of $7.

Facilities include a clubhouse with a limited pro shop where you can arrange for lessons and get help with tournament planning, an 18-tee driving range, plus a restaurant and lounge with banquet facilities.

Directions: Located north of downtown Auburn. Take 104th Avenue SE north .8 mile and go left on Green River Road. Follow 1 mile to the course.

Jade Greens Golf Course

9 Holes <> Par 34 <> Length 2656 yards <> $-$$

18330 SE Lake Holm Road <> Auburn, WA

253-931-8562 <> Reservations Available

www.jadegreens.com

The Jade Greens course surrounds 30 acres of natural wetlands. As you play you'll enjoy nice views of Mt. Rainier, the Cascade Mountains and the wetlands. Completed in 1989, the course is open year round.

The slope is 110 and the course rating 65. You'll find two tees at each hole. From the forward tees the total distance is 2232 yards.

Weekend green fees are $18 for 9 holes or $28 for 18 seven days a week. Seniors can play for $13 and $23. Juniors pay $11 and $19. Golf clubs rent for $10, pull carts are $2 and motorized carts $7.50 and $12.50.

Facilities include a restaurant where you can get cold beer and wine, plus a pro shop and driving range. The driving range has mat tees and you get a small bucket of balls for $4 or a large one for $7. Golf lessons and help with tournament planning are available.

Directions: Located east of downtown Auburn. Follow Highway 18 east and take the Auburn-Black Diamond Road exit. After .4 mile turn right on SE Auburn Black Diamond Road and drive .3 mile to SE Lake Hold Road, turn right and drive .5 mile to the course.

Washington National Golf Club

18 Holes ◇ Par 72 ◇ Length 7305 yards ◇ $$$

14330 SE Husky Way ◇ Auburn, WA

253-333-5000 ◇ Reservations Available

www.washingtonnationalgolf.com

Designed by John Fought, this is home to University of Washington golf teams. Opened in 2000, the course rating is 75.6 and the slope 141. This dry winter course can be a little noisy but the course conditions make it worthwhile. The terrain is flat with contours, the fairways open, there is lots of sand and good roughs to avoid and it is decently maintained.

All green fees include a cart; the rates Monday thru Thursday are $75 for 18 holes. On all major holidays and Friday thru Sunday it's $92. Get on the course before 8:00 am Monday thru Thursday and you can play for $65; twilight rates begin at 5:00 pm when everyone pays $50 seven days a week..

Facilities include a practice area, 30-tee driving range, community facilities, a full-service pro shop and a snack bar. At the range you'll pay $5.50 for a small bucket of balls or $10 for a big one.

Directions: Located east of Auburn; follow Highway 18 east 2 miles to the Auburn-Black Diamond Road exit. Turn right on SE Auburn-Black Diamond Road, go 2.5 miles, turn right on 152nd Avenue SE and after .7 mile turn right onto SE Husky Way.

(DuPont)

The Home Course

18 Holes ◇ Par 72 ◇ Length 7424 yards ◇ $$-$$$

2300 Hoffman Hill Blvd. ◇ DuPont, WA

253-964-0520

www.thehomecourse.com

The Home Course is gorgeous with snow-capped mountains, forested foothills and water views. It sits 200' above Puget Sound. You'll find five sets of tees here; from the forward tees the total distance is 5470 yards. The course rating is 76.4 with a slope of 138 from the back tees.

You'll find water, sand and trees and a terrain with rolling hills. Designed by Mike Asmundson, this course opened to rave reviews. Owned by the Washington State Golf Association, it has something for every level of golfer.

Green fees are $62 Friday thru Sunday as well as all major holidays and $52 the rest of the week. Seniors can play Monday thru Thursday for $40. Weekend twilight rates are $40, Monday thru Thursday they're $36.

Facilities include practice greens, a 20-tee driving range, a full-service pro shop and a clubhouse offering food and drink.

Directions: Located right on the water in DuPont.

(Fort Lewis)

Eagles Pride Golf Course

27 Holes <> Par 37
Length 3505 yards <> $-$$

Fort Lewis Army Base
Fort Lewis, WA

253-967-6522
Reservations Available

www.jblmmwr.com/golf_eagles_
pride.html

There are three 9-hole golf courses at Fort Lewis, and outstanding mountain views. This is primarily a military course but they can bring guests. Golf among towering trees on this scenic course; the terrain is varied with lots of sand and a little water.

In the winter they close one course and offer 18-hole play on the other two.

The three 9-hole layouts range in length from 3204 to 3505 yards and are par 35-37 depending on which course is played. This course was started in

1929. The 18-hole course was built as a WPA project and a third nine was added in 1979.

Green fees for non-military golfers are $20 for 9 holes or $35 for daily play. Twilight rates begin at 3:00 pm and rates drop to $20 for 18 holes until dusk. Golf clubs rent for $15 and $25, pull carts are $4 and motorized carts $8 and $15. Rates for military golfers vary based on rank and service.

Facilities include a limited pro shop and a 10-tee covered driving range. The base also has historic military equipment displays and a military museum.

Directions: Located at the Fort Lewis Army Base, just off I-5.

(Gig Harbor)

Madrona Links Golf Course

18 Holes ◇ Par 71 ◇ Length 5602 yards ◇ $-$$

3604 22nd Avenue NW ◇ Gig Harbor, WA

253-851-5193 ◇ Reservations Available

www.madronalinks.com

Madrona Links is open year round dawn to dusk and offers a flat, easy-to-walk terrain. Designed by Ken Tyson, the course opened in 1978 and has a rating of 63.7 and a 107 slope. Hazards include four lakes and dozens of sand traps. The Madrona trees are beautiful and deer often wander across this country course. Three sets of tees provide plenty of variety. The total distance from the women's tees is 4737 yards for par 73.

Friday thru Sunday and all major holidays green fees are $24 and $32. Monday thru Thursday golfers pay $20 and $27. Senior golfers can play on weekdays for $18 and $25. Juniors age 7 thru 17 pay $15 for 9 or 18 holes. Golf clubs rent for $15, pull carts $5 and motorized carts $16 and $30.

They have a pro shop, restaurant/lounge, banquet facilities and a driving range. The range is for irons only and has grass tees. You get range balls for $3 per token. Lessons and help with tournament planning are available.

Directions: Located south of downtown Gig Harbor. Follow Highway 16 toward Tacoma, take exit #9 toward the Tacoma Narrows Airport, go right onto 36th Street NW and take the first left onto 22nd Avenue NW.

(Puyallup)

Lipoma Firs Golf Course

27 Holes ◇ Par 36 ◇ Length 3420 yards ◇ $-$$

18615 110th Avenue E ◇ Puyallup, WA

253-841-4396 ◇ Reservations Available

www.lipomafirsgolfcourse.com

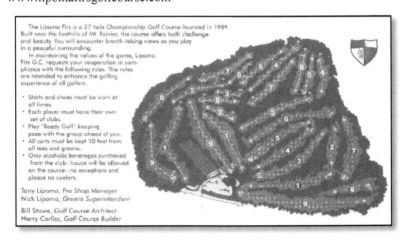

You'll find three 9-hole golf courses on this relatively flat course. This former Christmas tree farm has narrow, tree-lined fairways and some very challenging holes. It is a good winter course.

The slope is 116 and the course rating 69.7. The greens are large and there are enough sand bunkers to keep your aim sharp. From the ladies' tees the total distance is 5500 yards.

Designed by Bill Stowe, this course opened in 1989 and has terrific views of Mt. Rainier.

On weekends green fees go up to $30 for 18 holes; you'll pay $25 Monday thru Friday. Juniors and seniors can play 18 holes on non-holiday weekdays for $19.

Twilight rates are $17 on weekdays and $20 on weekends; time fluctuates based on when the sun goes down but fall twilight rates begin at 1:00 pm.

You can rent golf clubs for $10, pull carts are $4 and motorized carts are $16 for 9 holes or $24 for 18 holes. If you're the lone rider the cart is only $16 for 18 holes.

Facilities include practice greens and bunkers, a restaurant serving cold beer and wine, banquet facilities, a 20-tee driving range and a full-service pro shop. Lessons and help with tournament planning are available at the pro shop.

At the driving range you can get a small bucket of balls for $5 or a large bucket for $7.

Directions: Leave Highway 512 at the South Hill/Eatonville exit, go south for 6 miles, turn left at 187th and follow the signs to the golf course.

(Spanaway)

Classic Country Club

18 Holes ◇ Par 72 ◇ Length 6902 yards ◇ $$-$$$

4908 208th Street E ◇ Spanaway, WA

253-847-4440 ◇ Reservations Available

www.theclassicgc.com

Classic opened in 1991 and has over 60 sand bunkers, 30 grass bunkers and a couple of lakes to challenge your game. This course offers undulating fairways and large, well-protected greens. Hazards include sand, water and lots of trees. You'll find four tees at every hole. This dry winter course has lush green fairways and terrific views of Mt. Rainier. The slope is 134 and the course rating 73.2. From the forward tees the distance is 5656 yards.

Green fees on weekends and holidays are $29 for 9 holes or $49 for 18; weekdays you'll pay $29 or $39. Monday thru Friday juniors get a 40% discount, seniors and active military members a 20% discount. Twilight rates start at 3:30 pm seven days a week and everyone pays $17 and $25. Rates are lower off-season. Motorized carts rent for $10 and $15 per rider.

Facilities include a restaurant that serves beer and wine, banquet facilities, a full-service pro shop, driving range, snack bar, chipping and putting greens.

Directions: To find the Classic Country Club course leave I-5 at exit #127. Head east on Highway 512, turn right on Pacific Avenue, stay left when the road Y's and follow Highway 7 a short distance to 208th Avenue. Turn left and follow this to the course.

Lake Spanaway Golf Course

18 Holes ◇ Par 71 ◇ Length 7083 yards ◇ $$

15602 Pacific ◇ Spanaway, WA

253-531-3660 ◇ Reservations Available

www.lakespanawaygc.com

Lake Spanaway is county operated and open year round from dawn to dusk. This course was carved out of a fir forest, has large greens and enough doglegs and hazards to keep the game interesting.

The terrain is flat, the slope 125 and the course rating 73.5. Four sets of tees add variety to your game. From the women's tees the total distance is 5604 yards for par 74.

On weekends green fees are $26 for 9 holes or $39.75 for 18. On weekdays you'll pay $25 or $35. Active military members and seniors pay $18 and $27 Monday thru Friday and juniors play for $9 and $15. At twilight green fees for 18 drop to $25, the senior, junior and active military fees are $12 and $17 for 18 holes.

They have a clubhouse with a restaurant and lounge, banquet facilities, a full-service pro shop and a covered driving range. The range includes a green-tee box for woods and balls are $4-7.

Directions: Located in Spanaway on Pacific Avenue.

(Sumner)

Tapps Island Golf Course
9 Holes ◇ Par 35
Length 2670 yards ◇ $- $$

20818 Island Parkway E
Sumner, WA

253-862-7011
Reservations Available

www.tappsisland.net/new/golf

Tapps Island is a residential community with a pleasant semi-private 9-hole golf course. It has lots of water, some sand, plenty of tall trees and some slight hills plus a beautiful lakeside view of Mt. Rainier. From the women's tees the total distance is 4848 yards on this year-round course.

Green fees at Tapps Island are $23 for 9 holes and $35 for 18 on weekdays, $20 and $30 on weekends. Seven days a week juniors can play for $12 and $16, and seniors age 60 and older can play before noon for $14 and $20.

Golf clubs rent for $15 per 9, pull carts $8 and motorized carts $10 for 9 holes or $15 for 18.

You'll find a restaurant that serves beer and wine, banquet facilities and a full-service pro shop. Lessons and help with tournament planning are available at the pro shop.

Directions: Follow Highway 410 east 6.4 miles and turn left on 214th Avenue. After 1.8 miles this becomes 218th but it changes back to 214th after another 2.1 miles; .6 mile after this switch turn left onto Island Park Way. Take the first right onto 210th Avenue, the second right onto 28th Street and turn right onto 211th Avenue. Take the first right turn onto 30th, turn left on 210th Avenue East, right onto Island Park and follow to the golf course.

(Union)

Alderbrook Golf & Yacht Club

18 Holes <> Par 72 <> Length 6037 yards <> $-$$$

E 300 Country Club Drive <> Union, WA

360-898-2560 <> Reservations Available

www.alderbrookgolf.com

This course is open year round, weather permitting, and offers a gently rolling terrain that is easy to walk. Built in 1965, the front nine is flat but the back nine has some hills. You'll find a gorgeous view of the Olympic

Mountains, lots of trees and occasionally spot wildlife on this course. The slope is 115 and the course rating 70.3. You'll find five sets of tees. From the forward tees the total distance 4551 yards.

Green fees Monday thru Thursday are $25 for 9 holes or $40 for 18 and $35 and $55 Friday thru Sunday all summer long. Winter rates (November 15th thru the middle of February) is when you'll pay $15 and $20 early in the week, or $20 and $25 Friday thru Sunday. Spring and fall green fees are $20 and $30 Monday thru Thursday or $25 and $40 Friday thru Sunday. They rent clubs for $10-15 and motorized carts for $20 for 9 or $28 for 18.

Facilities include a clubhouse with a restaurant and lounge, banquet facilities, a full-service pro shop and a covered driving range. You can get help with tournament planning and lessons at the pro shop

Directions: Take Highway 106 for 8 miles and follow signs to course.

(This is the end of the Tacoma Area Listings)

Tukwila

Foster Golf Links

18 Holes ◇ Par 68 ◇ Length 4804 yards ◇ $-$$

13500 Interurban S ◇ Tukwila, WA

206-242-4221

www.fostergolflinks.com

The Duwamish River winds through the fairways at Foster Golf Links. Built in 1925 and operated by the city parks, this golf course is open year round.

The course is fairly flat with a few gentle rises and is challenging, yet easy. It's a good place for beginners and those looking for a quick game. The slope is 101 and the course rating 62.8. From the ladies tees the total distance is 4529 yards for par 70.

Green fees on weekends are $27 for 9 holes or $38 for 18; on weekdays it's $23 and $33. Seniors play on weekdays for $19 and $28, and juniors pay $10 and $16 seven days a week. Twilight rates begin two hours before sunset when you can play 9 holes for $15.

Motorized carts are $19 for 9 holes or $29 for 18. Facilities include a restaurant/lounge and a full-service pro shop.

Directions: Leave I-5 at the Marginal/Tukwila exit and head right .5 mile to the course.

Tumwater

Tumwater Valley Golf Course

18 Holes ◇ Par 72 ◇ Length 7038 yards ◇ $-$$

4611 Tumwater Valley Drive ◇ Tumwater, WA

360-943-9500 ◇ Reservations Available

www.tumwatervalleygc.com

Situated above the artesian wells made famous by the Olympia Brewery this course offers gorgeous mountain views. You could end up in the water on more than half the holes; a stream winds through the course and ponds dot its landscape. The fairways are fairly open, flat and easy to walk. The rating is 73.4 and the slope 118. From the forward tees the distance is 5428 yards.

Weekday green fees are $19 for 9 holes or $30 for 18. On weekends it's $21 and $40. The Early Bird Special happens before 8:00 am when everyone pays $15 for 18 holes during the week or $20 on weekends. There is a Twilight Special of $19 weekdays or $24 weekends for 18. The Super Twilight Special starts at 4:00 pm and weekday rates drop to $10 and on weekends to $15. Juniors play all week for $10 and seniors for $21.

Facilities include a restaurant/lounge with a banquet area, a driving range and pro shop. At the driving range it's $4.60 to $11.04 for a bucket of balls. Lessons and help with tournament planning are available at the pro shop.

Directions: Leave I-5 South at exit #103 and turn left over the highway. Take a right at the first stop light, left at the next light and follow this to the course. From I-5 North take exit #103 and turn right.

Vancouver

Fairway Village Golf Course

9 Holes ◇ Par 34 ◇ Length 2490 yards ◇ $-$$

15509 SE Fernwood Drive ◇ Vancouver, WA

360-254-9325 ◇ Reservations Available

www.ourfairwayvillage.org

The Fairway Village course slopes gently towards the river and is part of a 55+ residential community. Built in 1981, this golf course was designed by Bunny Mason and is open year round.

The slope is 103 and the course rating 64. From the ladies' tees the total distance is 2316 yards. You'll find plenty of mature trees, sand bunkers, a gently rolling terrain and quiet surroundings.

Green fees are the same seven days a week, $16 for 9 holes or $26 for 18 April thru October, $14 or $24 the balance of the year. Golf clubs rent for $10, pull carts for $3 and $6 and motorized carts are $15 for 9 holes or $25 for 18.

Fairway has practice putting and chipping greens, a practice range and a full-service pro shop where you can get help with tournament planning and sign up for golf lessons. Snacks are available in the pro shop.

Directions: Leave I-205 at the Camas exit, go east to 164th, north to McGilvrey and turn left after 3 blocks. You can follow the signs from there.

Lakeview Golf Challenge

9 Holes ◇ Par 27 ◇ Length 852 yards ◇ $

2425 NW 69th Street ◇ Vancouver, WA

360-693-9116 ◇ Reservations Available

Hole	1	2	3	4	5	6	7	8	9	Out	10	11	12	13	14	15	16	17	18	In	Total
Red	93	114	128	78	90	99	90	82	70	852	173	141	128	82	105	109	103	82	80	1,003	1,855
Men's Handicap																					
Men's Par	3	3	3	3	3	3	3	3	3	27	3	3	3	3	3	3	3	3	3	27	54
Women's Par										0										0	0
Women's Handicap																					

Lakeview is for golfers who want a real challenge. It's not supposed to be easy, it was designed to improve your short game and changes constantly. Open year round from 8:00 am to dusk, it has flat, rolling greens, two ponds and hundreds of trees.

Designed by Duke Wagner, it first opened in 1982. This course has a beautiful view of Vancouver Lake and the greens are contoured with difficult slopes. You'll find two sets of flags for playing 18 holes.

Green fees remain the same seven days a week, $12 for 9 holes or $20 for 18 holes. Seniors can play Monday thru Friday for $10 and $16.

This course operates on the honor system when no one is in the clubhouse, so be sure to bring exact change for the lockbox. Golf clubs rent for $5 and pull carts are $3. Motorized carts are not allowed on this course.

Facilities are minimal but you will find a putting green and chipping area and there is cold pop and some snacks at the clubhouse.

Directions: Leave I-5 North on 78th Street. Head west to Frit Valley Road, turn left, drive .7 mile and go right on Whitney. Follow this .5 mile to the course.

Pine Crest Golf Course

9 Holes ⬦ Par 27 ⬦ Length 1170 yards ⬦ $

2415 NW 143rd Street ⬦ Vancouver, WA

360-573-2051 ⬦ Reservations Available

www.pinecrestgc.net

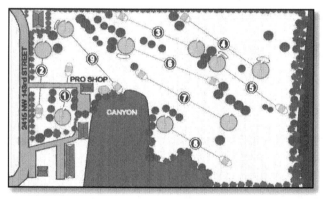

Pine Crest is a simple par 3 golf course with rolling hills, mature trees, sand bunkers and a great view of Mount St. Helens and Mt. Hood.

Overlooking Salmon Creek, the course facilities are open year round. Closing at dusk, they open at 7:00 am on weekends and 7:30 am the rest of the week.

Besides the creek there is also a canyon to avoid. Pine Crest has a certification program for 8-9 year olds, making it a great place to bring young golfers.

This is one of Washington's best bargains. During the week you can play 9 holes for $10; on weekends and holidays you'll pay $11.

Juniors play during the week for $7.75 and on weekend for $8.75. Seniors pay $8.75 seven days a week.

Pull carts are $3, golf clubs too. They have a Bavarian-style clubhouse where you can get snacks as well as cold pop and beer. Plus they also have a putting green.

Directions: Take the 134th Street exit off I-5, after 2 miles turn left onto 143rd Street and follow this to the course.

Woodland

Lewis River Golf Course

18 Holes <> Par 72 <> Length 6367 yards <> $$-$$$

3209 Lewis River Road <> Woodland, WA

360-225-8254 <> Reservations Available

www.lewisrivergolf.com

Lewis River is open year round from dawn to dusk unless closed by snow. This is a beautiful dry winter course and it has both flat and rolling terrain. The course has tree-lined fairways and well-contoured greens.

Built in 1966, this course began with 9 holes. It became an 18-hole course in 1969. Between 1996 and 2001 many changes were made to the course and facilities. The slope is 121 and the course rating 70.4. The women's tees have a total distance of 5286 yards for par 73.

Green fees for 18 holes at Lewis River are $47 on weekends and holidays, $37 the rest of the week. Twilight rates begin at 4:00 pm. On weekends and holidays you'll pay $30, the rest of the week $25.

Seniors and juniors can play on weekdays for $27; from November thru February juniors and seniors can play 9 holes for $30 on weekends or $15 on weekdays. Motorized carts are $16 when playing 9 holes or $30 for 18.

Facilities include a clubhouse, a restaurant and lounge with banquet facilities, a full-service pro shop and driving range. Lessons and help with tournament planning are available at the pro shop.

Directions: Take State Highway 503 east of town 5.5 miles. Go right after the Lewis River Country Store and turn right onto the golf course road.

Yelm

Nisqually Valley Golf Course

18 Holes ◇ Par 71 ◇ Length 6149 yards ◇ $-$$

15425 Mosman Street SW ◇ Yelm, WA

360-458-3332 ◇ Reservations Available

www.golf-courses.us/tag/yelm-golf-courses

This is a scenic course with an outstanding view of Mt. Rainier. The terrain is relatively flat with some hills and the course stays dry during the winter months.

Open year round, this course was built in 1976 and from the women's tees the total distance is 5693 yards for par 72. Hazards include water and sand. The greens are small but sloped and the fairways are fairly open.

Monday thru Friday green fees are $15 for 9 holes or $20 for 18. On weekends and holidays you'll pay $20 or $27.

Active military members and seniors can play Monday thru Friday for $12 when playing 9 holes or $17 for 18. Juniors pay $8 and $15 on weekdays and after 11:00 am on weekends.

Golf clubs rent for $8 and $12, pull carts are $3 and motorized carts $14 for 9 holes or $22 for 18.

Facilities include a restaurant and lounge with a banquet area plus a pro shop. At the pro shop they can help with lessons and tournament planning.

Directions: Located .5 mile south of downtown Yelm.

Region Three
Central Washington

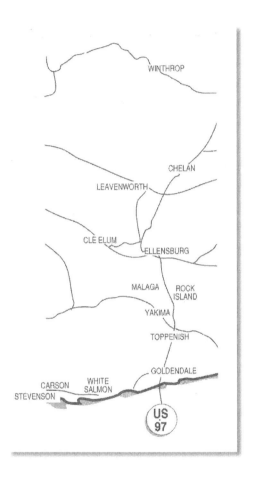

COURSES IN CENTRAL WASHINGTON

Central Washington is where you will find the state's newest golf courses. The Suncadia Rope Rider Golf Course in Cle Elum opened late in 2011 and is 7271 yards long from the back tees. Built on an old coal mine, the name pays tribute to the region's early miners who descended into these mines on ropes.

With the opening of this Cle Elum course Central Washington now sports four 18-hole golf courses longer than 7000 yards. Suncadia Rope Rider is the longest at 7271 yards.

Chelan's Bear Mountain Ranch Golf Course comes in a close second at 7231 yards and offers spectacular views of both the Columbia River and Lake Chelan.

Orondo's Desert Canyon Golf Resort is 7217 yards from the back tees and the Rock Island Golf Club is 7153 yards.

The city with the most golf courses in this region is Yakima with four courses. They have two 18-hole courses and two 9-hole courses. Yakima's Apple Tree Golf Course includes a century-old apple orchard; in the spring the flowering trees bring extra beauty to this 6892 yard 18-hole course.

The second 18-hole course, Suntides Golf Course, sits in a small valley and includes a couple of creeks bringing water into play on 13 holes. The first 9-hole course, Fisher Park Golf Course, is a 1354 yard par 3; the second, Westwood West Golf Course, is 2689 yards for par 35.

Central Washington golf courses showcase magnificent scenery too; you can golf above the Columbia River, play in high alpine meadows, or enjoy a round of golf surrounded by snow-capped mountains and forested hills. Malaga's Three Lakes Golf Course overlooks the Columbia River and the Skamania Lodge Golf Course is located in the Columbia River Gorge.

The Mt. Adams Country Club golf course in Toppenish has spectacular views of Mt. Adams, as does White Salmon's Husum Hills Golf Course. In Leavenworth the Kahler Glen Golf Course is high in the mountains and surrounded by forests and the Leavenworth Golf Club has the Wenatchee River running along two sides.

The following twelve cities in Central Washington have golf courses.

Chelan	Cle Elum
Ellensburg	Goldendale
Leavenworth	Malaga

Orondo

Rock Island

Stevenson

Toppenish

Winthrop

Yakima

Chelan

Bear Mountain Ranch Golf Course

18 Holes ◇ Par 72 ◇ Length 7231 yards ◇ $$-$$$

1050 Bear Mountain Ranch Road ◇ Chelan, WA

509-682-8200 ◇ Reservations Required

www.bearmt.com

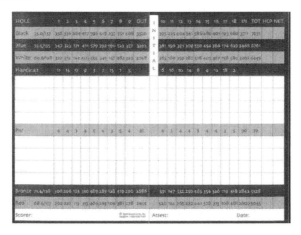

Bear Mountain Ranch overlooks the Columbia River and Lake Chelan in a gorgeous desert setting. Designed by Robert Yount and Don Barth, this course opened in 2005 and is part of a recreational community. It has well maintained fairways and greens.

The terrain rolls with the natural landscape on this 350-acre golf course and five sets of tees have been provided offering everything from a challenging 5063 yards or an extremely long 7231 yards. Water, and 60-70 sand bunkers, will test your aim.

The Bear Mountain Ranch Golf Course is a cart-only course so all green fees include a cart. From May to October green fees are $59 Monday thru Thursday and $89 the balance of the week.

Rates are reduced at 1:30 pm Monday thru Saturday and at 11:30 am on Sunday. Play then and save $10-30. Pre-season rates are $49 all week long, and post-season rates are $39-$59 depending on the day and time. Rental clubs are available.

Facilities include a full-service pro shop, a cafe serving hot food and cold beer, a putting green, chipping and practice bunker and a 25 tee driving

149

range. You'll find help with tournament planning and lessons at the pro shop.

Directions: Located southwest of town. Follow the road around the lower end of the lake to Bear Mountain Ranch Road. The course is about 5.4 miles from town.

Lake Chelan Golf Course

18 Holes ◇ Par 72 ◇ Length 6430 yards ◇ $-$$

Golf Course Road ◇ Chelan, WA

509-682-8026 ◇ Reservations Required

www.lakechelangolf.com

Hole	1	2	3	4	5	6	7	8	9	OUT	10	11	12	13	14	15	16	17	18	IN	TOT
	545	177	400	340	347	345	375	420	530	3279	406	155	275	336	490	410	376	510	173	3151	6430
	530	157	385	320	335	330	359	420	500	3136	406	150	260	318	490	390	376	490	150	3022	6158
Par	5	3	4	4	4	3	4	3	5	36	4	3	4	4	5	4	4	5	3	36	72
	5	3	4	4	4	3	4	5		36	4	3	4	4	5	4	4	5	3	36	72
	3	17	5	13	9	11	15	7	1		12	18	14	16	6	4	8	2	16		
	465	150	345	310	332	325	338	365	455	2865	285	150	230	300	400	390	345	440	85	2635	5500

The Lake Chelan course offers an outstanding view of the lake against a backdrop of towering mountains. The front nine holes are flat; the back nine are hilly. Built in 1970, this course is open mid-March thru October. From the women's tees it's a total distance of 5500 yards. The course rating is 71.2 and the slope 126.

From Memorial Day weekend thru September green fees are $25 for 9 holes or $42 for 18. Twilight rates are $20 and $29. After 2:00 pm Monday thru Thursday juniors and seniors can play 9 holes for $17 or 18 for $24.

The rest of the year regular green fees are $22 for 9 holes or $34 for 18 and twilight rates are $18 and $26. Juniors and seniors play Monday thru Thursday after 2:00 pm for $15 and $21. Golf carts rent for $14 when playing 9 holes or $28 for 18. Rental clubs and handcarts are available.

Facilities include a driving range, a restaurant where you can get cold beer and wine plus a banquet area and fully-stocked pro shop. Lessons and tournament planning help are available.

Directions: Take Manson Highway northwest and follow the signs to the golf course. It is less than 2 miles from the center of town.

Cle Elum

Suncadia Rope Rider Golf Course

18 Holes ◇ Par 71 ◇ Length 7271 yards ◇ $$-$$$
3600 Suncadia Trail ◇ Cle Elum, WA
509-649-6400 ext. 6 ◇ Reservations Available
www.suncadiaresort.com

There are two 18-hole courses at Suncadia but only the Rope Rider course is open to the public. Designed by Peter Jacobsen and Jim Hardy, it is built on an old coal mine and the name is a tribute to early miners.

Opened in August of 2011, the terrain is gently rolling and there's lots of water, sand and big trees. Doglegs and greens backed up to water make it a challenging place to play. Tees at a variety of distances make it a good place for all levels. From the forward tees the total distance is 5001 yards.

Green fees depend on the time of day you play, day of the week and season; weekends and holidays are the more expensive rate shown. June thru September 18 holes will cost you $69-99 from 7:00 am to 8:00 am, $79-129 from 8:00 am to 1:00 pm, $69-99 between 1:00 p.m. and 3:00 pm, and $49-69 from 3:00 pm until close. To play 9 holes the fee is $40-60.

Off-season rates are $54-74 between 7:00 am and 8:00 am, $64-89 from 8:00 am to 1:00 pm, $54-74 between 1:00 p.m. and 3:00 pm, and $49-59 from 3:00 pm until closing. To play 9 holes it is $30-40. All rates include a motorized cart and range balls for the practice range. Juniors can play any time the course is open for $40. Clubs rent for $60.

Deluxe accommodations, spa packages and fine dining are all found at the resort. A short game practice area, putting greens and three chipping greens are all being added to the Rope Rider course. You can get help with tournament planning and lessons at the pro shop.

Directions: Located northwest of Cle Elum. Follow Highway 903 to the golf course road. It's about 4 miles from town.

Sun Country Golf Course

18 Holes ◇ Par 71 ◇ Length 5715 yards ◇ $$-$$$

841 St. Andrews Drive ◇ Cle Elum, WA

509-674-2226 ◇ Reservations Available

www.golfsuncountry.com

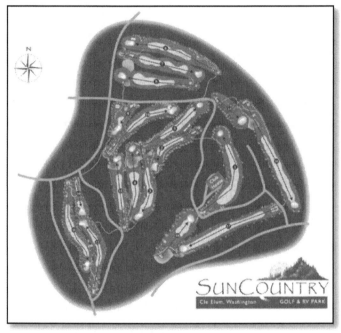

This challenging course is located in the beautiful Upper Kittitas Valley. A high-mountain alpine course, it is open April 15 thru October 15. Weekend hours are 6:00 am to dusk. On weekday they open at 7:00 am.

The slope for men is 119 and the rating 68.8. For women it's 124 and 70.9. There are two sets of tees so golfers can play 18 holes with some variety. The ladies par is 72 for a total distance of 5503 and there's plenty of water and trees to keep your aim straight.

Friday thru Sunday you'll pay $30 for 9 holes or $42 for 18. After 3:00 pm Sunday thru Thursday it drops to $22 and $30. Clubs rent for $10, pull carts are $5 and motorized carts $10 per person for 9 holes or $14 if playing 18. The trail fee when you bring your own cart is $10.

Facilities include a limited pro shop, a snack bar where you'll find sandwiches and cold beer, plus a driving range. At the pro shop they can help you with tournament planning. Banquet facilities are available.

Sun Country also has its own RV park.

Directions: Leave I-90 at exit #78 on Golf Course Road and follow this south to St. Andrews, turn left and go to the bottom of the hill.

Ellensburg

Ellensburg Golf Club

9 Holes ◇ Par 35 ◇ Length 2988 yards ◇ $-$$

3231 S Thorp Highway ◇ Ellensburg, WA

509-962-2984

This semi-private course doesn't open to the public until 1:00 pm on weekends. The rest of the time it's available to the public. Located along the Yakima River, it was built in the 1930s and has a lovely mountain view.

Weather permitting they are open March thru mid-November. The rating is 35.9 and the slope 115. The women's par is 73 for a total distance of 2807 yards. The greens are small and the fairways wide but the wind can be a major factor in your shot at this course.

During the week green fees are $12 for 9 holes or $22 for 18. On weekends and holidays you'll pay $13 and $23.

Clubs rent for $5, pull carts are $1 and motorized carts are $10 per 9 holes.

Facilities include a pro shop, 24-tee driving range, restaurant, lounge, and banquet facilities. At the pro shop they can help with tournament planning and arrange for lessons.

At the driving range you'll pay $2-5 for a bucket of balls. Driving range hours are 7:00 am to 7:00 pm, but they stay open until dusk during the summer.

Directions: Take I-90 to town, across the river, and follow to the course.

Goldendale

Goldendale Country Club

9 Holes ◇ Par 36 ◇ Length 2850 yards ◇ $$

1901 N Columbus Avenue ◇ Goldendale, WA

509-773-4705 ◇ Reservations Advised

www.goldendalegolf.com

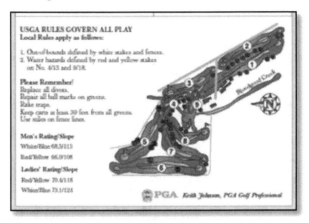

This is a semi-private club but anyone who lives more than 15 miles outside of the Goldendale city limits can play for daily fees every day but Thursday. Thursday is reserved for members only.

The course has wonderful scenic views of Mt. Hood, Mt. Adams and Mount St. Helens.

The greens are small but interesting and are kept in good shape. A creek comes into play twice. Open year round, weather permitting, the course has two sets of tees. The women's par is 37 for a total distance of 2546 yards.

Green fees are the same seven days a week, $20 for 9 holes or $30 for 18. Winter rates are $10 and $20.

They rent golf clubs for $10, pull carts are $4 and motorized carts $12.50 for 9 holes or $25 for 18.

Facilities include a full-service pro shop, banquet room and a limited snack bar offering cold pop and beer.

Help with lessons and tournament planning is available at the pro shop.

Directions: Take the Broadway exit at Goldendale. Drive 1 mile west to the flashing yellow light, turn right and go 1.5 miles to the course.

Leavenworth

Kahler Glen Golf Course

18 Holes <> Par 70 <> Length 5579 yards <> $$-$$$

20890 Kahler Drive <> Leavenworth, WA

509-763-4025 <> Reservations Available

www.kahlerglen.com

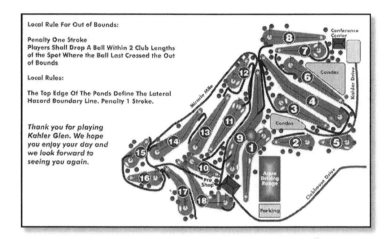

The terrain is mountainous and surrounded by a natural forest. Designed by Randy Pelton, the slope is 118 and the rating 67.1. Lots of water, tight fairways, sand and natural hazards will keep you on your toes. Open the end of April thru October, from the red tees the distance is 4737 yards.

Green fees Monday thru Thursday are $35-50 with a cart Monday thru Thursday or $28-35 if walking. After 2:00 pm it is $35 and $25. Holidays and Friday thru Sunday it is $44-59 with a cart or $35-44 if walking.

Twilight Rates are $42 and $35. Juniors who play with a paying adult play for $10-20. Clubs rent for $15.

Facilities include a driving range, overnight accommodations, a snack bar that serves beer and a full-service pro shop. Lessons and help with tournament planning are available at the pro shop.

Directions: Leave Highway 2 on Highway 207. Drive 4 miles and follow the Kahler Glen Golf Course signs.

Leavenworth Golf Club

18 Holes ⬦ Par 71 ⬦ Length 5699 yards ⬦ $-$$$

9101 Icicle Road ⬦ Leavenworth, WA

509-548-7267 ⬦ Reservations Needed

www.leavenworthgolf.com

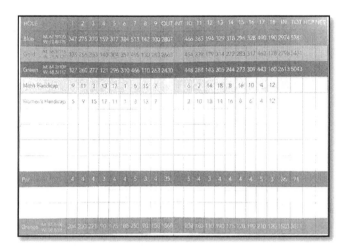

This course sits in the mountains outside the Bavarian-style town of Leavenworth and is surrounded on two sides by the Wenatchee River. The scenery is gorgeous and wildlife, including an occasional bear, is common on the fairways.

Open April thru October, depending on snowfall, the terrain is one of rolling hills. Built in 1947, the slope is 112 and the rating 66.8. The total distance from the red tees is 5241 yards.

Green fees Monday thru Thursday are $21 for 9 holes or $35 for 18. The rest of the week and on holidays you'll pay $30 and $48. Twilight rates start at 1:01 pm when green fees Friday thru Sunday are $22 and $37. It's $15 and $25 the rest of the week. Carts are $9 for 9 holes or $16 for 18.

Facilities include a restaurant, open 7:00 am to 8:00 pm, a fully-stocked pro shop and banquet facilities. Lessons are available.

Directions: Located 1 mile west of town. Take Highway 2 to Icicle Road then .6 mile south.

Malaga

Three Lakes Golf Course

18 Holes ◇ Par 69 ◇ Length 5319 yards ◇ $-$$

2695 Golf Drive ◇ Malaga, WA

509-663-5448 ◇ Reservations Available

www.threelakesgolf.com

Built in 1953, the Three Lakes Golf Course is open year round. This course is hilly and challenging with tree-lined fairways that overlook the Columbia River. The surrounding area is full of orchards, making it a gorgeous place to play in the spring.

Weekday green fees are $17 for 9 holes or $30 for 18. On the weekend you'll pay $21 and $35. Juniors play during the week for $8 and $11 and on weekends for $13 and $17. Twilight rates begin at 2:00 pm in the spring and 4:00 pm in the summer when adults pay $20 during the week and $25 on weekends. Motorized carts rent for $10 per rider when playing 9 or 18 holes.

Facilities include a pro shop, a restaurant serving beer and wine, plus a banquet area and a grass driving range. At the range you'll pay $4-6 for a bucket of balls, depending on how many you need. You'll find help with lessons and tournament planning at the pro shop.

Directions: Malaga, and the Three Lakes Golf Club, is located 4 miles east of Wenatchee. Follow the Malaga-Alcoa Highway for 4 miles and turn at the Three Lakes Golf Club sign.

Orondo

Desert Canyon Golf Resort

18 Holes <> Par 72 <> Length 7217 yards <> $$-$$$

1201 Desert Canyon Blvd. <> Orondo, WA

509-784-4173

www.desertcanyonresort.com

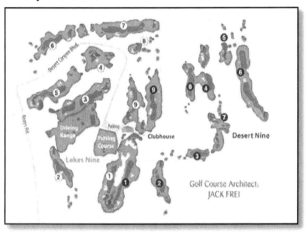

The Desert Canyon Resort is gorgeous and the course follows the natural terrain. Designed by Jack Frei and Rick Fehr, each hole has five sets of tees. The forward tees have a distance of 4939 yards, so there is enough variety for all levels of players. The resort dress code is enforced on course. Opened in 1993, the slope is 134 and the rating 73.9.

All green fees include a shared cart; walkers are not allowed. From mid-May thru September you'll pay $69 Monday thru Thursday before 1:00 pm, $49 after 1:00 pm and $39 after 3:00 pm. Friday thru Sunday it's $89, $59 after 1:00 pm and $39 after 3:00 pm. Seniors can play Monday thru Thursday before 8:30 am for $49. Juniors play for $29 during the week and $39 Friday thru Sunday. They also have an 18-hole putting course. Adults pay $12 but juniors and seniors only $9.

Pre-season rates are $32-$55 early in the week, $39-59 Friday thru Sunday, and is based on the time of day you play. Post-season rates range from $29-49 on weekdays, or $29-59 Friday thru Sunday.

Facilities include deluxe accommodations offering stay and play packages, a first-class restaurant, sports bar, driving range and a full-service pro shop. On the driving range you'll find 25 tees and pay $6 for a bucket of balls.

Directions: Leave Highway 97 at milepost 221 just north of Orondo on Bray's Road. Follow this 1 mile to Desert Canyon Blvd. and the course.

Rock Island

Rock Island Golf Club

18 Holes ◇ Par 72 ◇ Length 7153 yards ◇ $-$$

314 Saunders Road ◇ Rock Island, WA

509-884-2806 ◇ Reservations Available

www.Rockislandgolfcourse.com

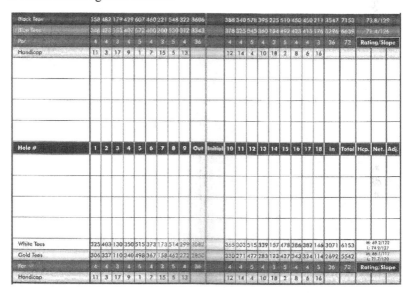

Black Tees		358	462	179	429	607	460	221	548	322	3606		388	340	578	395	225	510	450	450	211	3547	7153	73.8/129	
Blue Tees		346	428	163	407	572	400	200	530	312	3343		378	325	545	360	184	492	423	415	176	3296	6639	71.4/126	
Par		4	4	3	4	5	4	3	5	4	36		4	4	5	4	3	5	4	4	3	36	72	Rating/Slope	
Handicap		11	3	17	9	1	7	15	5	13			12	14	4	10	18	2	8	6	16				
Hole #		1	2	3	4	5	6	7	8	9	Out	Initial	10	11	12	13	14	15	16	17	18	In	Total	Hcp.	Net. Adj.
White Tees		325	403	130	350	515	373	173	514	299	3082		365	303	515	339	157	478	386	382	146	3071	6153	M: 69.2/122 L: 74.9/127	
Gold Tees		306	337	110	340	498	367	158	462	272	2850		330	271	477	283	123	427	343	324	114	2692	5542	M: 66.7/117 L: 71.7/120	
Par		4	4	3	4	5	4	3	5	4	36		4	4	5	4	3	5	4	4	3	36	72	Rating/Slope	
Handicap		11	3	17	9	1	7	15	5	13			12	14	4	10	18	2	8	6	16				

The Rock Island course is open year round, weather permitting. It has a nice mountain view, flat terrain and plenty of water to make the game challenging. The course rating is 73.8 and the slope 129.

The greens are large and the fairways wide at Rock Island. The 13th hole is the signature hole. A par 4, it has a large water hazard as well as a nice dogleg. The 14th hole is short but that same pond makes it a testy par 3. The total distance from the forward tees is 5542 yards.

Green fees are $16.50 for 9 holes or $26.00 for 18 Monday thru Thursday and $18.50 and $35.00 Friday thru Sunday. The Twilight Special is $12.50 and $22.00. Clubs rent for $4-15, pull carts $6 and motorized carts $7.50 per seat on 9 holes or $14 per seat for 18.

Facilities include putting and chipping greens, a restaurant with a banquet area and a clubhouse with a nice pro shop where you can get help with tournament planning and lessons.

Directions: Located just outside East Wenatchee. Follow Highway 28 southeast of Wenatchee. It's 9.5 miles to the Rock Island Course.

Stevenson

Skamania Lodge Golf Course

18 Holes ◇ Par 70 ◇ Length 5776 yards ◇ $$$

1131 Skamania Lodge Way ◇ Stevenson, WA

541-427-2541 ◇ Reservations Suggested

www.skamania.com

Designed by Bunny Mason, this course opened in 1993 and operates February thru November. Cut out of a forest and overlooking the Columbia River Gorge you'll find spectacular views. The rolling terrain includes natural areas and wildlife ponds. One pond contains a beaver lodge and a few holes wrap around the ponds.

Winter hours are 9:00 am to 5:00 pm and they're open 7:00 am to 8:00 pm the balance of the year. The 3rd hole is protected by Lilly Pad Lake, #8 is considered the toughest on the course, and the wind can affect several holes taxing your skills. From June thru September green fees are $79.00 before 2:00 pm and $59 after 2:00 pm.

During October it's $59 until noon but only $49 after. In November it's $49 but seniors play for 25% off and juniors for 50% off regular rates. February thru April it's $49 and in May before noon it's $59 and after noon $49. Clubs rent for $15 and $20 for a standard set, $30 and $45 for a premium set.

Facilities include accommodations with a discount for golf, a practice bunker, chipping and putting greens, a restaurant and a coffee shop that serves beer and wine plus a full-service pro shop and driving range. Help with tournament planning and lessons are available.

Directions: Take Highway 14 west of Stevenson, turn left onto Rock Creek Road and follow this to the lodge and golf course.

Toppenish

Mt. Adams Country Club

18 Holes ◇ Par 72 ◇ Length 6341 yards ◇ $$-$$$

1250 Rocky Ford Road ◇ Toppenish, WA

509-865-4440 ◇ Reservations Available

www.mtadamsgolf.com

White Tees	295	460	392	208	479	379	306	172	293	2984		373	417	520	530	389	371	138	392	147	3277	6261				70.1/123
Handicap	10	2	6	16	4	8	12	18	14			5	3	7	1	9	13	17	11	15						
Hole #	1	2	3	4	5	6	7	8	9	Out	In/Hol	10	11	12	13	14	15	16	17	18	In	Total	Hcp	Net	Adj
Red Tees	261	446	363	156	447	373	287	127	248	2708		360	388	448	441	304	373	315	368	136	2951	5707				72.8/127
Handicap	10	4	12	16	2	14	8	18	6			9	1	5	3	7	13	19	11	17						

This semi-private course has only a $5.00 Social Membership Fee so it's included. Flat with gentle draws, it offers a spectacular view of Mt. Adams. The course has some of the most playable greens in Central Washington and is open March thru November.

Private members play on Wednesday and Thursday mornings until 1:00 pm but the rest of the time the course is open to the public. It opens at 7:00 am

161

on weekdays and 6:00 am on weekends. The women's tees have a total distance of 5873 yards for a par of 73.

Public players first must pay the $5 annual fee; after that green fees are $16 for 9 holes or $39 for 18. On weekdays it's 18 holes for $28. Seniors, age 65 and older can play during the week for $16 and $26.

Facilities include a limited pro shop, a restaurant and lounge with banquet facilities and a driving range. Lessons and help with tournament planning are available at the pro shop.

Directions: Located 2 miles south of Toppenish via Highway 97.

Winthrop

Bear Creek Golf Course

9 Holes ◇ Par 36 ◇ Length 3114 yards ◇ $-$$

19 Bear Creek Golf Course Road ◇ Winthrop, WA

509-996-2284 ◇ Reservations Recommended

www.bearcreekgolfcourse.com

Bear Creek is pretty with snow-capped mountains in the distance, especially in the fall when the colors are changing. The course is challenging. Some holes are on the hillside and others in the meadow. Your ball has to travel across the lake on one hole.

The back nine plays like a different course, the tee placement is so varied. The slope is 117 and the rating 68.9 for men, 69.4 for women. The women's par is 37 for 2706 yards. You can play here April thru October, depending on the snowfall, from 8:00 am to dark.

Green fees during the week are $17 for 9 holes or $29 for 18. On the weekend you'll pay $20 and $32. Tuesdays seniors play for $15 and $25 and juniors for $10 and $18. Motorized carts are $10 per 9 holes, pull carts $5.00 and you can rent clubs for $10-20.

Directions: Located 3 miles south, along Eastside County Road.

Yakima

Apple Tree Golf Course

18 Holes ◇ Par 72 ◇ Length 6892 yards ◇ $$-$$$

8804 Occidental Avenue ◇ Yakima, WA

509-966-5877 ◇ Reservations Needed

www.appletreeresort.com

The 17th hole at Apple Tree sits on a tiny apple-shaped island. Opened in 1992, this challenging course is located on the site of a 100-year-old apple orchard and very scenic. The terrain is relatively flat with some hills and weather permitting you can golf here year round from sunrise to sunset. The slope is 124 and the ratings 70.7 for men or 72.0 for women. The women's par is 72 for 5857 yards.

Summer green fees are $39 for Yakima residents and $54 for others Monday thru Thursday. The rest of the week residents pay $54 and others $69. Early bird and twilight specials bring reduced rates. Juniors and seniors can play for discounted rates during the week.

Winter fees are $33 on weekends and holidays or $28 Monday thru Thursday. During spring it's $37 for residents and $47 for non-residents Monday thru Thursday and $47 and $57 Friday thru Sunday. Clubs rent for $25 for a standard set or $45 for premium, pull carts $10 and power carts $16 per person per 9 holes. Bring your own cart and the trail fee is $10.

Facilities include a wonderful restaurant, full-service pro shop and a driving range with grass tees. Balls are $6-10 for a bucket at the range. Lessons are available at the pro shop and they can help with tournament planning as well.

Directions: Located in west Yakima. Take the 40th Ave. exit off Highway 12 and go south to Washington Avenue, turn left at 64th Avenue and right on Occidental.

Fisher Park Golf Course

9 Holes <> Par 27 <> Length 1354 yards <> $

823 S 40th Avenue <> Yakima, WA

509-575-6075

www.yakimaparks.com/parks/fisher-park-golf-course

Built in 1961, this course is open March thru October between dawn and dusk. Fisher Park is beautifully landscaped with well kept greens and lots of evergreens and flowers. The terrain is easy to walk.

Green fees are $9.25 for 9 holes or $14.75 for 18 all week long. Juniors and seniors pay $8.25 and $12.75.

Families, 2 adults and 2 juniors, can all play for $26; 2 adults with 1 junior pays $21. On Tuesdays women play 9 holes for $7 and on Thursdays men play for $7. Clubs rent for $5.75 and pull carts $3.25.

Facilities include a putting green and a small pro shop where you'll find snacks and soft drinks. Lessons are available.

Directions: Located in west Yakima, across from the high school.

Suntides Golf Course

18 Holes ◇ Par 70 ◇ Length 5941 yards ◇ $-$$

231 Pence Road ◇ Yakima, WA

509-966-9065 ◇ Reservations Available

www.suntidesgolf.com

Open year round, Suntides is nestled in a small valley and has two creeks that bring water into play on 13 of the 18 holes. The terrain is flat and easy to walk with some elevated tees. The women's par is 71 for a total distance of 5509 yards.

Green fees are the same seven days a week, $12 for 9 holes or $27 for 18. Clubs rent for $5 and $8, handcarts $2 and $4 and motorized carts $7 per person for 9 holes or $13 per person for 18.

Facilities include an 18-hole putting course, restaurant/lounge, banquet area, RV park, pro shop and driving range. At the driving range you can get a small bucket of balls for $3.50 or a large one for $6. Visit the pro shop for help with tournament planning and lessons.

Directions: Located 3 miles west of Yakima, via Highway 12.

Westwood West Golf Course

9 Holes ◇ Par 35 ◇ Length 2689 yards ◇ $

6408 Tieton ◇ Yakima, WA

509-966-0890 ◇ Reservations Available

Tee	1	2	3	4	5	6	7	8	9	Out
H/C	0	0	0	0	0	0	0	0	0	
Par	4	3	3	4	4	4	4	4	5	35
White	284	157	150	395	315	343	317	305	425	2691

Open dawn to dusk year round, unless heavy snow falls, this course was designed by Curly Hueston and built in 1964. It has a both hilly and flat fairways plus two sets of tees. The slope is 107 and the rating 32.5. The distance from the ladies' tees is 2607 yards.

Mondays seniors play for $12 and all else $16. On Tuesday everyone plays for $12 each. Wednesday thru Sunday all players pay $16. Clubs rent for $10, pull carts $3 and electric carts $12 for 9 holes.

Facilities include a pro shop, chipping and putting greens, a covered driving range with mat tees and a putting green. Snacks and cold pop are available at the pro shop. They can also help with tournament planning and lessons. On the driving range you'll pay $5.50 for a small bucket of balls or $7.50 for a large bucket.

Directions: You'll find this golf course by heading west of town along Tieton Drive.

Region Four
Eastern Washington

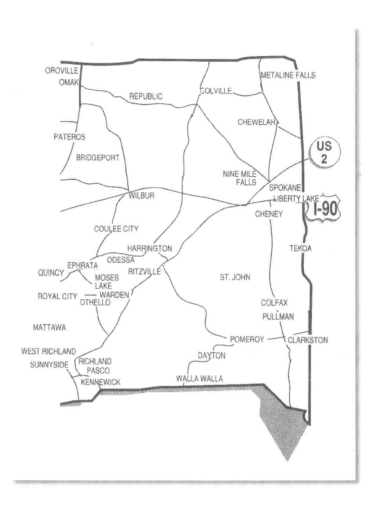

COURSES IN EASTERN WASHINGTON

Eastern Washington, with lots of public and semi-private golf courses and plenty of sunshine is a golfer's dream. Over half of these are 18-hole courses and one location has both an 18-hole course and a 9-hole course.

And, there are some pretty long 18-hole courses on the far eastern side of the state. Four have over 7000 yards from the back tees. In Walla Walla the Wine Valley Golf Club course at 7360 yards is the longest. Pullman's Palouse Ridge course is 7308 yards, Richland's Horn Rapids Golf Course 7060 yards and Canyon Lakes has a total distance of 7000 yards.

The longest 9-hole course is Hylander Greens in Moses Lake; from the back tees the total distance is 3774 yards. Pine Acres Par 3 in Spokane is the region's shortest 9-hole course at 760 yards. The oldest golf course in eastern Washington is a 9-hole course and was built in 1927.

There are lots of good bargains among these eastern Washington courses but Metaline Falls' Pend Oreille Golf Club has them all beat at $2-3 for 9 holes. In fact this is the cheapest course in the entire state of Washington.

Two of this region's golf courses have expanded from 6-hole courses into full-fledged 9-hole golf courses. They are the Serendipity Golf Course in Ione and the St. John Country Club course. In 2002 the Dominion Meadows Golf Course in Colville expanded from 9 to 18 holes.

The following cities in Eastern Washington have golf courses.

Bridgeport	Cheney
Chewelah	Clarkston
Colfax	Colville
Coulee City	Dayton
Ephrata	Harrington
Ione	Kennewick
Liberty Lake	Mattawa
Metaline Falls	Moses Lake
Nine Mile Falls	Odessa
Omak	Oroville
Othello	Pasco
Pateros	Pomeroy
Pullman	Quincy

Richland

Royal City

St. John

Tekoa

Warden

Wilbur

Ritzville

Spokane

Sunnyside

Walla Walla

West Richland

Bridgeport

Lake Woods Golf Course

9 Holes <> Par 35 <> Length 2841 yards <> $-$$

232 Half-Sun Way <> Bridgeport, WA

509-686-5721

www.lakewoodssgc.com

Lake Woods Golf Course is considered one of the best 9-hole golf courses in Washington. The terrain includes a few hills, lots of trees, narrow fairways, excellent greens, and is bordered by the Columbia River. Built in 1963, two sets of tees are available. The slope is 115 and the course rating 33.4. Lake Woods is open from mid-March thru October and also takes memberships.

Green fees are $17 for 9 holes or $28 for 18 Friday thru Sunday and holidays. The rest of the week it's $15 or $24. Students and active military can play 9 holes for $9 or 18 for $14. Golf clubs rent for $6 ($3 if you're a student) and pull carts are $3. Motorized carts are $13 for 9 holes or $22 for 18. The trail fee if you bring your own cart is $8.

Facilities include a chipping green, a cafe with hot food and cold beer, plus a limited pro shop where you can get help with tournament planning. At the driving range you'll find 10 grass tees and get a small bucket of balls for $3.

Directions: Located near Bridgeport State Park.

Cheney

The Fairways West Terrace Golf Course

18 Holes ◇ Par 72 ◇ Length 6408 yards ◇ $-$$

9810 W Melville Road ◇ Cheney, WA

509-747-8418 ◇ Reservations Available

www.golfthefairways.com

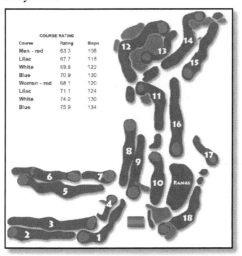

You'll find lots of water and quick true greens at The Fairways West Terrace Golf Course. This course opened in 1987 and is closed only when snow is on the ground. The terrain is slightly rolling, the slope 130, and the course rating 70.9. The women's tees have a slope of 120 and a rating of 68.1. This course travels thru natural wetlands and offers a mix of challenging holes.

Weekend green fees are $29 but after noon you can play 9 holes for $18.50. Tuesday thru Friday you'll pay $24 for 18 holes. On Mondays you can play for $19. Juniors and seniors play for reduced rates during the week and after noon on weekends. Twilight rates begin at 4:00 pm when everyone plays for $19. Pull carts rent for $4 and motorized carts are $16 for a lone rider or $26 for 18 holes. Bring your own cart and the trail fee is $9.

Facilities include a putting and chipping green, a restaurant and lounge with a banquet area and outdoor patio, full-service pro shop and driving range. At the pro shop they can help with tournament planning and arrange lessons.

Directions: Located east of I-90. Take exit #272 and go right on Hayford Road, left on Melville and follow this to the course.

Chewelah

Chewelah Golf Club

27 Holes ◇ Par 72
Length 6645 yards ◇ $-$$

2537 E Sand Canyon Road
Chewelah, WA

509-935-6807
Reservations Available

www.chewelahgolf.com

Chewelah has lots of trees, is flat and easy to walk. You'll find a couple of lakes and some sand, making it a pleasant place to play.

This semi-private course is open from April thru mid-November and offers three sets of tees. From the women's tees the total distance is 4406 yards.

All year long walking rates Monday thru Thursday are $17 for 9 holes, $30 for 18 holes, or $35 to play all 27. Friday thru Sunday it will cost you $20, $35 and $40.

Seniors get a $5 discount on Mondays and Tuesdays; juniors not only save $5 on Mondays and Tuesdays but can also get a $10 discount on 18 or 37 holes.

Clubs rent for $8, $15 and $20, pull carts are $3-4 and a motorized cart will add $5-20 to your total cost. Twilight rates begin at 2:00 pm.

Facilities include the Rusty Putter, a bar and grill with banquet facilities, plus a driving range, RV park and a full-service pro shop where you can get help with lessons and tournament planning.

At the driving range a bucket of balls is $5-8.

Directions: Leave Highway 395 on Sand Canyon Rd and go 3 miles.

Clarkston

Quail Ridge Golf Course

18 Holes ◇ Par 71 ◇ Length 5603 yards ◇ $-$$

3600 Swallows Nest Drive

509-758-8501 ◇ Reservations Available

www.golfquailridge.com

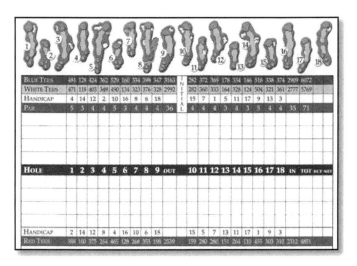

	1	2	3	4	5	6	7	8	9	OUT		10	11	12	13	14	15	16	17	18	IN	TOT	HCP	NET
Blue Tees	481	128	424	362	529	160	334	398	347	3163		282	372	369	178	334	146	516	338	374	2909	6072		
White Tees	471	118	403	349	490	134	323	376	328	2992		282	360	353	164	326	124	506	321	361	2777	5769		
Handicap	4	14	12	2	10	16	8	6	18			15	7	1	5	11	17	9	13	3				
Par	5	3	4	4	5	3	4	4	4	36		4	4	4	3	4	3	5	4	4	35	71		
Hole	1	2	3	4	5	6	7	8	9	OUT		10	11	12	13	14	15	16	17	18	IN	TOT	HCP	NET
Handicap	2	14	12	8	4	16	10	6	18			15	5	7	13	11	17	1	9	3				
Red Tees	388	100	375	264	465	129	268	353	198	2539		159	280	280	151	264	130	455	303	310	2312	4851		

The original nine was built in 1971 and a second nine added in 1992. The slope is 120 and rating 69.0. It has a gently rolling terrain, some water and small greens. From the women's tees it's 4720 yards. It offers a view of the Snake River and Blue Mountains and is open year round 6:00 am to dusk in the summer and 7:00 am in winter.

Green fees are $18 for 9 holes or $29 for 18 when walking. With a cart it's $28 and $44. Motorized carts are $8 per seat for 9 or $14 for 18. The trail fee is $7 when you bring your own cart. Winter rates are offered December and January and are $25 for 9 holes or $25 for 18.

Facilities include a restaurant/lounge, banquet area and a covered patio overlooking the 10th hole. They also have a full-service pro shop, practice putting green and a driving range with mat tees. They offer help with tournaments and arrange lessons at the pro shop.

Directions: Located 4 miles south of Clarkston. Take Highway 129 south, turn on Critchfield Road and head west to the course.

Colfax

Colfax Golf Club

9 Holes ◇ Par 35 ◇ Length 3010 yards ◇ $-$$

2402 Cedar Street ◇ Colfax, WA

509-397-2122 ◇ Reservations Recommended

www.colfaxgolf.com

Built in 1927 and open year round, sunup to dusk, the slope is 117 and the rating 67.8. Located beside the Palouse River it's a flat yet challenging course with sand traps and trees. The women's par is 36 for 2817 yards. Open at 7:00 am April thru September; October thru March they don't open until noon Wednesday thru Sunday and are closed Monday and Tuesday.

Green fees are the same seven days a week, $15 for 9 holes or $22 for 18. You can rent clubs for $5, pull carts $2 and motorized carts are $13 for 9 holes or $20 for 18. Facilities include a clubhouse, full bar and pro shop.

Directions: Take Highway 195 north to Cedar Street; located less than 2 miles from the center of town.

Colville

Dominion Meadows Golf Course

18 Holes ◇ Par 72 ◇ Length 6743 yards ◇ $-$$

1861 E Hawthorne ◇ Colville, WA

509-684-5508

www.colvillegolf.com

In 2002 Dominion Meadows reopened as an 18-hole course. The new back nine has lots of water and links-style golfing in a valley framed by mountains. Open April thru October, weather permitting, the terrain is rolling, there are plenty of trees and golfers often spot wildlife while playing. The terrain is fairly challenging, the course has a slope of 125 and a rating of 72.3. The total distance from the women's tees is 4869 yards.

Green fees at Dominion are $21 for 9 holes or $29 for 18 on weekends. Seniors can play for $17 and $24. During the week adults pay $19 and $26 and juniors $9 and $13.

They have a full-service pro shop where you can arrange for lessons and get help with tournament planning. Banquet facilities and a driving range are also found on site.

Directions: Turn at the first stoplight and go to the top of the hill.

Coulee City

Sun Lakes Resort Golf Course

9 Holes ◇ Par 35 ◇ Length 3123 yards ◇ $

34228 Park Lake Road NE ◇ Coulee City, WA

509-632-5738

www.sunlakesparkresort.com

Hole	1	2	3	4	5	6	7	8	9	Out	Total
White	484	360	342	188	407	155	442	286	176	2,840	2,840
Blue	511	388	375	226	434	170	448	316	195	3,063	3,063
Men's Handicap	10	10	10	10	10	10	10	10	10		
Men's Par	5	4	4	3	4	3	5	4	3	35	35
Women's Par	5	4	4	3	4	3	5	4	3	35	35
Women's Handicap	6	8	1	7	4	5	2	9	3		

The Sun Lakes Resort Golf Course is part of Sun Lakes Park Resort. Built in 1949 it is open from March thru October. This is a beautiful course overlooking Sun Lakes, rocky bluffs and scenic canyons. The course terrain is hilly and wildlife is often spotted on the fairways. From the women's tees the total distance is 2702 yards.

During the week green fees are $13 for 9 holes or $17 for 18. On weekends you'll pay $15 and $19. Juniors age 9 and under can play 9 holes for $8 during the week or $12 on weekends and holidays. Golf clubs rent for $7, pull carts are $4 and power carts are $14 for 9 holes or $22 for 18.

Facilities include a putting green, overnight accommodations, an RV park, cafe and a small pro shop where you can get help with tournament planning. They also sell snacks and cold drinks.

Directions: Located 6 miles south of Coulee City on Highway 17.

Dayton

Touchet Valley Golf Course

9 Holes <> Par 36 <> Length 2931 yards <> $-$$

209 N Pine Street <> Dayton, WA

509-382-4851

This course is located in the beautiful Touchet River Valley, southeastern Washington's gateway to the Blue Mountains. Hazards include sand, water and a horse racing track.

Open from daylight to dusk, March thru October, the terrain is nice and flat. Four sets of tees are available.

This is considered a pasture-style course and was originally built on an old dairy farm in 1910. The slope is 122 and the course rating 35.5.

Weekend green fees are $18 for 9 holes or $21 for 18; on weekdays it's $15 and $17. Students get great discounts. Grades K-8 pay $8 and $10 weekdays, $10 and $12 on weekends. High school students pay $10 and $12 Monday thru Friday and $12 and $14 on Saturday and Sunday.

Golf clubs rent for $5, pull carts are $3 and motorized carts rent for $15 and $20. They have a limited pro shop, plus a restaurant and lounge with banquet facilities.

Directions: Located 1 block north of Highway 12 at Dayton's west end, in the center of the Columbia County Fairgrounds Race Track.

Ephrata

Oasis Park Par 3

9 Holes ◇ Par 27 ◇ Length 930 yards ◇ $

2541 Basin SW ◇ Ephrata, WA

509-751-5102

www.oasisrvandgolfcourse.com

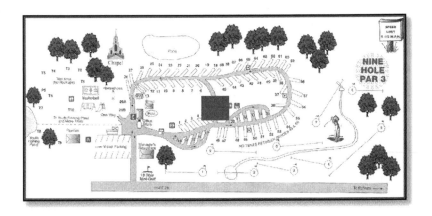

Golf is both affordable and challenging at the Oasis Park Par 3 golf course. The terrain is flat with some hills, plenty of water, landscaped fairways, banked greens and grass tees.

Open dawn to dusk year round they only close this course occasionally for bad weather. This quiet location also has a miniature golf course as well as this executive par 9.

You can play 9 holes for $10 or all day for $15. If you're under age 16, or older than 60, you can play 9 holes for $8 and the all day rate is $12. Clubs rent for $3 and handcarts are $2. On the miniature golf course everyone pays $3 to play and a putter is included.

Facilities include an RV park with tent and RV sites and a limited pro shop where you can get help with tournaments and lessons.

Directions: Located 1 mile south of Ephrata, on Highway 28.

Harrington

Harrington Golf & Country Club

9 Holes ◇ Par 36 ◇ Length 3166 yards ◇ $

700 S Second ◇ Harrington, WA

509-253-4308 ◇ Reservations Available

Harrington is a semi-private course but the public is welcome any time. Open March thru October, it has wide fairways, big greens, trees and doglegs. The slope is 119 and the course rating 35. The total distance from the women's tees is 2983 yards for a par of 37. Designed by Bob Putman, this course opened in 1962.

All week long green fees are $13 for 9 holes or $18 for 18 holes. Seniors can play for $11 and $16. Juniors play for $8 and $12. Motorized carts rent for $13 and $23. Bring your own cart and the trail fee is $6.

Facilities include a seasonal cafe with banquet facilities, a 20-tee driving range and full-service pro shop.

Directions: Located right in Harrington.

Ione

Serendipity Golf Course

9 Holes ◇ Par 31

Length 1781 yards ◇ $-$$

N 30992 LeClerc Road

Ione, WA

509-442-4653

Reservations Available

www.harringtonbiz.com/golf
course.htm

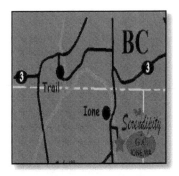

This course is a 9-hole course that began as a private 6-hole course but was later expanded. Designed by Scott Ramsey, this executive course is short and flat but it has some difficult greens. Two ponds and a creek add challenge and the greens are tight and fast. The longest hole is 315 yards, the shortest 101. From the red tees the total distance is 1549 yards.

Situated in the Selkirk Mountains the views are nice with mountains all around and the beautiful Pend Oreille River running alongside. Open dawn to dusk, wildlife spotted on the course include deer, elk, eagle and osprey.

Green fees are the same all week long, $15 for 9 holes or $25 for 18. Motorized carts rent for $20. There is a Spring Special where green fees are $10 and $15 and a cart is included.

Directions: Located in the town of Ione along Highway 31.

Kennewick

Canyon Lakes Golf Course

18 Holes ◇ Par 72 ◇ Length 7000 yards ◇ $$-$$$

3700 W Canyon Lakes Drive ◇ Kennewick, WA

509-582-3736 ◇ Reservations Available

www.canyonlakesgolfcourse.com

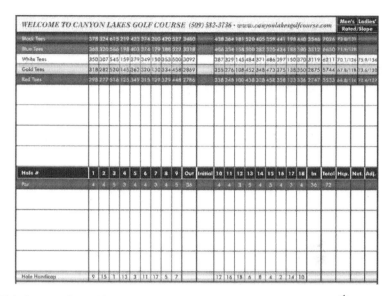

This is one of Washington's highest rated golf courses and its 12th hole has the distinction of being the largest green in the Northwest. Weather permitting, you can play year round at Canyon Lakes. The slope is 127 and the ratings 73.4 for men, 72.0 for women.

This course has rolling fairways, fast greens, numerous bunkers and lakes. Designed by John Steidel, it opened in 1981. The women's tees have a total distance of 5700 yards.

Green fees Monday thru Thursday are $54 for 18 holes, on Friday you'll pay $59, and on weekends and holidays $64. Juniors pay $45. You can play 9 holes on weekends and holidays for $54. Monday thru Friday you'll pay $49 and after twilight $38.

Pull carts rent for $5, golf clubs $20 and power carts $12 per person when playing 9 holes or $20 per person on 18.

Facilities include the Duck Pond Restaurant and Bar plus a snack bar, driving range and pro shop. Lessons and help with tournament planning are available at the pro shop.

On the driving range you'll find grass tees and you can get a bucket of balls for $4-7 depending on the size of the bucket desired. They also have an 18-hole putting course. Everyone pays $5 to play this miniature course.

Directions: Follow Highway 395 south to 27th Avenue. The golf course road is just east of the highway.

Columbia Park Golf Course

18 Holes ◇ Par 55 ◇ Length 2447 yards ◇ $

2701 Columbia Park Trail ◇ Kennewick, WA

509-586-2800 ◇ Reservations Available

www.playcolumbiapark.com

	1	2	3	4	5	6	7	8	9	OUT	10	11	12	13	14	15	16	17	18	IN	TOT	HCP	NET
Men's Yardage	157	101	95	189	146	153	127	69	130	1145	125	348	129	172	249	130	155	91	123	1302	2447		
Men's Par	3	3	3	3	3	3	3	3	3	27	3	3	3	3	4	3	3	3	3	28	55		
Men's Handicap	4	10	14	2	12	16	6	18	8		5	17	11	3	1	15	9	13	7				
HOLE	1	2	3	4	5	6	7	8	9	OUT	10	11	12	13	14	15	16	17	18	IN	TOT	HCP	NET
Ladies' Yardage	157	101	95	189	146	153	127	69	130	1145	125	348	129	172	249	130	155	91	123	1302	2447		
Ladies' Par	3	3	3	3	3	3	3	3	3	27	3	3	3	3	4	3	3	3	3	28	55		
Ladies' Handicap	4	10	14	2	12	16	6	18	8		5	17	11	3	1	15	9	13	7				
Score:									Attest:									Date:					

The Columbia Park course is on the Columbia River and the summer view is one of hydroplane races and water skiers. Designed by Rocky Dorsett and open mid-February thru mid-November this is an easy-to-walk course. It will challenge players of all skills but is a good place for beginning players and family groups.

During the week 9 holes are $13 or 18 are $18. On weekends the rates go up to $15 and $20. Seniors 50 and older are $10 and $12.50 during the week, $13 and $17.50 on weekends. Juniors younger than 17 pay $8 and $11 Monday thru Friday, $11 and $14 on weekends. Twilight begin at 3:00 pm; on weekdays it's $11 and weekends $12. Super twilight begins at 5:00 pm and fees drop to $9 and $10.

They have a snack bar, a 20-tee driving range and a limited pro shop where you can get help with tournament planning and arrange for lessons. The driving range is open from 8:00 am to dusk, has grass tees, and you get 35 balls for $4, 70 for $7 or 105 for $9.

Directions: Located next to the Columbia River. Leave US 395 at Highway 240 and take the park exit. The course is 3.5 miles from downtown Kennewick.

Tri-City Country Club

18 Holes ◇ Par 65 ◇ Length 4900 yards ◇ $$-$$$

314 N Underwood ◇ Kennewick, WA

509-783-6014 ◇ Reservations Required

www.tccountryclub.com

This tree-lined semi-private course is open to the public and one of the oldest courses in the Tri-Cities. Originally constructed in 1938 with help from the WPA, it has rolling hills, water and plenty of mature trees to block the spring winds.

The 14th tee offers a spectacular view of the course as well as the Columbia River and the Blue Mountains. Open year round, three sets of tees are available. The course rating is 63.7 and the slope 113 from the blue tees. The course is closed on Monday mornings for maintenance.

Public green fees are $40 for 18 holes Monday thru Thursday and $50 Friday thru Sunday and on holidays. Juniors play for $20 seven days a week and seniors get to play for twilight rates.

Twilight rates for everyone else begin at 4:30 pm; you'll pay $35 on holidays and Friday thru Sunday, $30 the rest of the week. Motorized carts are $15 per rider.

They have a free practice range, a restaurant and lounge with banquet facilities and a full-service pro shop. They can help you with tournament planning and lessons at the pro shop.

Directions: From downtown Kennewick, follow West Kennewick Avenue 1.3 miles to the course entrance on Underwood Street.

Liberty Lake

Liberty Lake Golf Course

18 Holes ◇ Par 70 ◇ Length 6607 yards ◇ $$

24403 E Sprague Avenue ◇ Liberty Lake, WA

509-255-6233 ◇ Reservations Available

www.libertylakewa.gov/246/Golf

Open year round weather permitting you'll find four lakes, white sand bunkers and a remodeled clubhouse. The front nine is nice and long; the back nine is shorter with rolling hills and lots of trees. The fairways are tight, the slope 128 and the rating 71.1. From the women's tees the par is 74 for a total distance of 5006 yards.

Monday thru Thursday it's $22 for 9 holes or $30 for 18. Before 3:00 pm Friday thru Sunday and on all holidays green fees are $28 and $34. After 3:00 pm you'll pay $28 whether you play 9 holes or 18. Seven days a week juniors can play for $9 and $15. A $30 discount card will save you money if you play Spokane County courses often.

Facilities include a 15-tee grass driving range, sand bunker chipping area, putting green, clubhouse, restaurant and lounge, plus and a full-service pro shop. Lessons can be arranged at the pro shop.

Directions: Leave I-90 at Liberty Lake exit and go south to Sprague Avenue. Turn left and follow road 1 mile; the course is on the left.

Meadowwood Golf Course

18 Holes <> Par 72 <> Length 6874 yards <> $$

24501 E Valley Way <> Liberty Lake, WA

509-255-9539 <> Reservations Available

www.visitspokane.com/listings/MeadowWood-Golf-Course/10772

Meadowwood was built in 1988 and designed by Robert Muir Graves. This municipal golf course is open from mid-March thru mid-November and it has 7 lakes, 52 large bunkers and a rolling terrain. Covering 148 acres, the slope is 129 and the rating 72.4. The total distance from the women's tees is 5880 yards.

Monday thru Thursday you'll pay $21 for 9 holes or $27 for 18. Before 3:00 pm Friday thru Sunday and on holidays green fees are $21 and $29. After 3:00 pm it's $29 whether you play 9 holes or 18.

All week juniors play 9 or 18 holes for $15. A $30 discount card saves you lots of money if you play Spokane County courses often.

Facilities include a sand chipping area, putting green, clubhouse with a restaurant and bar, full-service pro shop, and a 9-acre water driving range. Lessons and help with tournament planning are available.

Directions: From I-90 take exit #296 and continue to Liberty Lake Drive. Follow this to Country Vista Boulevard, Molter and Valley Way. The course is 1 mile down Valley Way.

Trailhead at Liberty Lake Golf Course

9 Holes ◇ Par 31 ◇ Length 2072 yards ◇ $-$$

1102 N Liberty Lake Road ◇ Liberty Lake, WA

509-928-3484 ◇ Reservations Available

www.libertylakewa.gov/golf

Designed by Denny Reger, this course opened in 1973 and was formerly known as Valley View. It is open March thru December weather permitting. The terrain is easy to walk and the area surrounded by rolling hills. It offers a beautiful view of the mountains and has two sets of tees so you can play 18 with variety.

Weekday green fees are $16 for 9 holes or $23 for 18. During the week and after 2:00 pm on weekends and holidays golfers younger than 18 or over age 65 can play for $10 and $14. On weekends and holidays after 2:00 pm everyone pays $14.

Golf clubs rent for $10, pull carts $4 and power carts are $14 for 9 holes or $28 for 18 holes.

You'll find a restaurant/lounge with banquet facilities, a full-service pro shop and driving range. The range offers buckets of balls for $6-9. Lessons as well as help with tournament planning are available.

Directions: Located right off I-90 in Liberty Lake.

Mattawa

Desert Aire Golf Course

18 Holes <> Par 72 <> Length 6501 yards <> $-$$

505 Clubhouse Way W <> Mattawa, WA

509-932-4439

www.daoa.org

Desert Aire is a semi-private course with no restrictions on public play. Open year round, they have a slightly hilly terrain and a view that includes the Columbia River.

This is a well-groomed course with natural desert roughs. The back nine opened in 1993 and the front nine in 1972. The slope is 111 for men and 115 for women and the ratings 69.9 and 71.9. From the ladies' tees it's 5786 yards for par 73.

Weekday fees are $19 for 9 holes or $33 for 18. On weekends and holidays it's $25 and $39. Juniors play for $8 and $14. Seniors age 62 and older pay $17 or $31 on weekdays and $23 or $37 weekends.

You rent golf clubs for $12, pull carts are $2-3 and motorized carts $7.50-12.50 per seat. November thru March green fees drop to $12 and $24 Monday thru Thursday and $16 and $28 the rest of the week. They have a full-service pro shop and a driving range.

Directions: Located 5 miles south of Mattawa, on Highway 243.

Metaline Falls

Pend Oreille Golf Club

9 Holes ◇ Par 31 ◇ Length 2183 yards ◇ $

Golf Course Road ◇ Metaline Falls, WA

509-446-2301

www.pasturegolf.com/courses/pendoreille

This is one of the cheapest place to golf in the Pacific Northwest. Located in the state's northeastern corner, this rugged course is surrounded by forest. The terrain is flat with some hills, the fairways fairly wide and the greens sand. Wildlife is occasionally seen on the fairways.

The official season is May thru September when the grounds are maintained by volunteers. This is pasture golf and operates on the honor system.

During the week green fees are $2 during the week and $3 on weekends.

There is no rental equipment and you must have exact change for the green fee box.

Directions: Located off Highway 31, about 3 miles north of town.

Moses Lake

The Links at Moses Pointe

18 Holes ◇ Par 72 ◇ Length 7549 yards ◇ $$-$$$

4524 Westshore Drive ◇ Moses Lake, WA

509-764-2275 ◇ Reservations Available

www.mosespointe.com

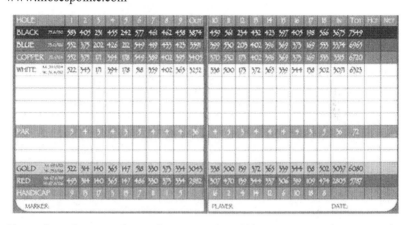

Situated on the west shore of Moses Lake, this resort course is open to the public January thru early October. With six sets of tees you'll find plenty of variety. The slope is 130 and the rating 75.6. From the forward tees the distance is 5787 yards. You'll find plenty of sand, several small ponds and some good doglegs on this course.

Green fees late April thru early October are $27 for 9 holes, $36 with a cart, Monday thru Thursday. 18 holes are $44 and $59. Friday thru Sunday you'll pay $54 for 18 holes, $69 with a cart.

Off-season rates are lowest January thru mid-March; 9 holes without a cart will cost $21 and 18 holes $29 early in the week, Friday thru Sunday you'll pay $24 and $34. Junior and senior discounts are available.

Facilities include a nice restaurant and lounge plus banquet facilities and a pro shop.

Directions: From the I-90 Moses Lake exit simply head north 4 miles on Westshore Drive.

189

Hylander Greens Golf Course

9 Holes ◇ Par 27 ◇ Length 3774 yards ◇ $

1475 Nelson Road NE ◇ Moses Lake, WA

509-766-2757 ◇ Reservations Available

www.highlandergc.com

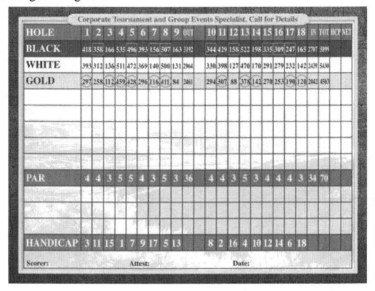

Corporate Tournament and Group Events Specialist. Call for Details

HOLE	1	2	3	4	5	6	7	8	9	OUT	10	11	12	13	14	15	16	17	18	IN	TOT	HCP	NET
BLACK	418	358	166	535	496	393	156	507	163	3192	344	429	158	522	198	335	309	247	165	2707	5899		
WHITE	393	312	136	511	472	369	140	500	131	2964	330	398	127	470	170	291	279	232	142	2439	5403		
GOLD	297	258	112	459	428	296	116	411	84	2461	294	307	88	378	142	270	253	190	120	2042	4503		
PAR	4	4	3	5	5	4	3	5	3	36	4	4	3	5	3	4	4	4	3	34	70		
HANDICAP	3	11	15	1	7	9	17	5	13		8	2	16	4	10	12	14	6	18				

Scorer: Attest: Date:

Highlander Greens is flat, easy to walk and surrounded by trees. Built in 1991 there is no water on the fairways. Open year round weather permitting, early golfers can get at 6:00 am. From the ladies' tees the par is 29.

Formerly known as the South Campus Golf Course, this is part of the South Campus Athletic Club.

At this par 3 course you can play 9 holes for $14 or 18 for $17 seven days a week. Juniors age 17 and younger pay $10 for 9 holes or $12 for 18. Seniors age 63 and older pay the same rate.

Clubs rent for $5, pull carts $3 and motorized carts $15 for 9 holes or $18 for 18. You'll find a limited pro shop inside the athletic club, a 15-tee driving range and some snack and pop machines. Lessons and help with tournament planning are available at the pro shop. The driving range charges $3-5 for a bucket of balls.

Directions: Leave I-90 at exit #179 on Highway 17, turn right onto East Nelson Road and follow this to the course.

Nine Mile Falls

Sun Dance Golf Course

18 Holes ⋄ Par 70

Length 6000 yards ⋄ $-$$

9725 N Nine Mile Road
N Nine Mile Falls, WA

509-466-4040

www.sundancegc.com

The tree-lined fairways and small greens provide quite a challenge. Its terrain is relatively flat and easy to walk but a couple of sharp doglegs will test your distance shot. The women's par is 72 for a total distance of 5900 yards. They are open mid-March thru November.

Green fees are $20 or $27.50 weekends and holidays. Seniors play for $19 or $23 and juniors for $17 for 9 or 18 holes.

On non-holiday Mondays it's $14.50 for everyone. Tuesday thru Friday it's $18 and $24 with seniors paying $15 and $20 and juniors $15.

Twilight begins at 3:00 pm and everyone pays $14.50 and $16.50. A power cart adds $15-30.

Facilities include a restaurant/lounge, pro shop and driving range.

Directions: From Spokane take Francis Avenue. This becomes Nine Mile Road. The course is 2.5 miles further.

Odessa

Odessa Golf Club

9 Holes ⋄ Par 36 ⋄ Length 3094 yards ⋄ $-$$

13080 Highway 28 ⋄ Odessa, WA

509-982-0093 ⋄ Reservations Available

Tee	1	2	3	4	5	6	7	8	9	Out
H/C	4	8	12	18	14	2	6	16	10	
Par	4	4	5	3	4	5	3	4	4	36
Blue	367	366	461	178	329	516	197	317	363	3094
Red	367	360	383	160	329	418	140	317	363	2837
Par	4	4	5	3	4	5	3	4	4	36
H/C	4	8	12	18	14	2	6	16	10	

Built in 1967, this course is open mid-February thru mid-November weather permitting. The terrain has a few rolling hills but is easy to walk. The slope is 121 and the rating 36.2. There are wide fairways, elevated greens and a few sand traps. The distance from the women's tees is 2894 yards for a par of 37.

Weekday green fees are $13 for 9 holes or $20 for 18. On weekends it's $15 and $22. Seniors 60+ save $2 off the 18-hole rate. Juniors age 13 thru 18 get the same discount. Little ones play for $5.

Rental clubs are $3, handcarts $2 and motorized carts $11 for 9 holes or $22 for 18. Facilities include a putting and chipping area, practice bunker, pro shop with snacks and cold beer and an RV park.

Directions: Located at the west end of Odessa.

Omak

Okanogan Valley Golf Club

9 Holes <> Par 35
Length 3209 yards <> $-$$

105 Dankar Cutoff Road
Omak, WA

509-826-9902
Reservations Required

www.okanoganvalleygolf.com

The Okanogan Valley course was built in 1946 is open from the middle of March thru October. It has a fairly flat terrain. This is an interesting course with wide fairways, lots of trees and small greens.

You'll find a water hazard on the 7th hole and the 9th hole is considered the course's signature hole. It is par 5 with a dogleg and a total distance of 540 yards. Two sets of tees let you play 18. The slope is 119 and the rating 70.5. Wednesday afternoons the course is reserved for men only and Thursday mornings ladies only.

Green fees all week long are $18 for 9 holes or $28 for 18. During March rates drop to $10 and $18. Motorized carts are $14 and $26. You'll find a small pro shop, snack bar and cold beer. Lessons are available and so is a small banquet area for tournament celebrations.

Directions: Situated on a flat above Omak, at the south end of the reservoir. Simply follow the signs from town.

Oroville

Oroville Golf Club

9 Holes ◇ Par 36 ◇ Length 2926 yards ◇ $-$$

3468 Oroville/Loomis Road ◇ Oroville, WA

509-476-2390 ◇ Reservations Available

www.orovillegolfclub.com

The course opened in 1960, offers river views and is surrounded by mountains. The terrain is hilly and they are only open March thru October. This semi-private course is well-maintained, the fairways are narrow and the greens are good. Two sets of tees are available. The women's par is 37, the course rating is 33.9 and the slope 113.

Weekdays you'll pay $20 for 9 holes or $30 for 18. Weekends it's $25 and $35. You can rent clubs for $7, handcarts $3 and motorized carts $14 or $22. Facilities include a practice bunker, chipping green and a full-service pro shop with a snack bar and cold beer.

Directions: Located 2 miles west of Oroville via Nighthawk Road.

Othello

Othello Golf Club

9 Holes ◇ Par 35 ◇ Length 3066 yards ◇ $-$$

2269 W Mockingbird Lane ◇ Othello, WA

509-488-2376

www.othellogolf.com

The Othello Golf Club is located in the heart of the Columbia Basin and open year round. It provides a good challenge, a fairly flat terrain and easy to walk. The course is kept in great condition and has two sets of tees. A pond comes into play on the 9th hole. The course rating is 37.0 and the slope 123. Designed by John Reimer it opened in 1965. This course can be played from mid-February until mid-November.

On Saturday and Sunday it's $16 for 9 holes or $26 for 18. Weekdays you can play for $15 or $26 and juniors play for $10 and $15. Golf clubs rent for $7.50, pull carts $3 per 9 holes and motorized carts $15 for 9 holes or $26 for 18.

They have a putting green, chipping area, a restaurant and lounge with banquet facilities, a full-service pro shop, snack bar and a 40-tee driving range. You can get help with tournament planning at the pro shop. The driving range has grass tees and a bucket of balls is $4.

Directions: Head south on Bench Road for 1 mile, then west for 2 miles on West Mockingbird Lane.

Pasco

Pasco Golfland

9 Holes ◇ Par 27

Length 1131 yards ◇ $

2901 N Road 40
Pasco, WA

509-544-9291

www.Pascogolfland.com

This course opened in 1992 and was designed by Bill McIntyre. Golfland's par 3 layout is fun for all skill levels and a good place to work on your skills. There is a large driving range on site, which makes it a good training course.

Green fees remain the same all week long, $13 for 9 holes or $20 for 18. Seniors age 60 and older can play 9 holes for $12. Juniors age 18 and under play for half their age. Golf clubs rent for $3, pull carts are $3 and motorized carts $6 for 9 holes or $9 for 18.

Facilities include a large-capacity driving range plus a putting and chipping areas. A bucket of balls at the driving range will cost you $4 for 40 balls, $7 for 80, or $10 for 120 balls.

Directions: Golfland is found 3 miles northwest of downtown Pasco. Follow West Court Street. The course is located north of I-182, near the airport.

Sun Willows Golf Course

18 Holes ◇ Par 72
Length 6715 yards ◇ $$-$$$

2535 N 20th Avenue
Pasco, WA

509-545-3440
Reservations Available

www.playsunwillows.com

Sun Willows has dozens of bunkers and several lakes. Located in the heart of the Tri-Cities it offers a challenging back nine. The terrain is fairly flat, the greens medium sized and the course open year round weather permitting.

Three sets of tees are available. The distance from the ladies tees is 5695 yards. Designed by Robert Muir Graves the course rating is 72.0 and the slope 117.

Green fees are the same year round. Monday thru Thursday you'll pay $25 for 9 holes or $34 for 18, on Fridays $29 and $38 and on weekends and holidays $33 and $43. Monday thru Thursday seniors can play 18 holes for $31 and juniors pay $18.

Pull carts rent for $3 and motorized carts are $14 per person.

Facilities include a practice and chipping green, restaurant/lounge with a banquet area plus a 20-tee driving range and a full-service pro shop. You can get help with tournament planning and lessons at the pro shop.

A bucket of balls at range will cost you $2, $4 or $6 depending on how many needed.

Directions: Leave I-182 at the 20th Street exit and go north to Sun Willows Golf Course.

Pateros

Alta Lake Golf Club

18 Holes ◇ Par 72 ◇ Length 6678 yards ◇ $-$$

140 Alta Lake Road ◇ Pateros, WA

509-923-2359 ◇ Reservations Advised

www.altalakegolf.com

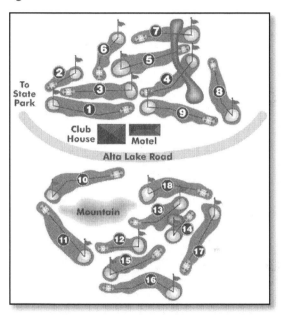

The front nine was built in 1975 and the back nine in 1993. The slope is 124 and the rating 72.5. Open March thru October it is situated in the Methow Valley and has lots of trees plus a gorgeous view of Alta Lake and the Columbia River.

A big creek cuts across three fairways making you drive across water and a pond sits between the 13th and 14th holes. The total distance from the women's tees is 5535 yards.

Monday thru Thursday green fees are $14.50 for 9 holes or $26 for 18. The rest of the week and holidays it's $18.50 and $35.

Clubs rent for $10, push carts $4 and $6 and motorized carts $14 and $26. If you're playing all day you can rent a push cart for $10 or a power one for $40.

Facilities include overnight accommodations, a nice clubhouse where you'll find a limited pro shop and a snack bar that sells cold beer. Other facilities include a motel and swimming pool.

Directions: Take Highway 53 off Highway 9, turn left on Toppenish Road and follow this to Alta Lake Road and the course.

Pomeroy

Pomeroy Golf Club Crystal Springs

9 Holes ◇ Par 31 ◇ Length 2033 yards ◇ $

1610 Arlington Street ◇ Pomeroy, WA

509-843-1197

Tee	1	2	3	4	5	6	7	8	9	Out
H/C	0	0	0	0	0	0	0	0	0	
Par	3	3	4	4	3	3	3	4	4	31
Mens	154	203	327	281	196	121	212	294	245	2033
Ladies	154	203	327	281	196	121	194	294	207	1977
Par	3	3	4	4	3	3	3	4	4	31
H/C	0	0	0	0	0	0	0	0	0	

This city course was built in 1932, has beautiful scenery and is open year round. It has large greens, well kept fairways and a hilly terrain that is fairly easy to walk.

You'll have to shoot up the hill on the 6th hole and down again on the 7th hole but it helps to keep the game interesting. The slope is 100 and the course rating 31.6. The total distance from the women's tees is 1977 yards for a par of 32.

Green fees are $13 or $19 all week long. From November thru March this course operates on the honor system so bring exact change. April thru

October they have some clubs, handcarts and motorized carts available for rental. Motorized carts rent for $10 per 9 holes.

You'll find a seasonal pro shop and a snack bar open April thru October. They can help with tournament planning at the pro shop.

Directions: Located 3 blocks off Main Street, near the city park.

Pullman

WSU Palouse Ridge Golf Club

18 Holes ◇ Par 72 ◇ Length 7308 yards ◇ $$$

1260 NE Palouse Ridge Drive ◇ Pullman, WA

509-335-4342

www.palouseridge.com

Designed by John F. Harbottle III, this 315-acre course has a rating of 75.9 and a slope of 140. The greens are interesting and kept in good condition and the total distance from the ladies' tees is 5106 yards. The terrain is primarily flat, with some nice hills, has lots of sand, one pond and a pleasant view.

When this course layout opened in 2009 both Golfweek and Golf Digest Magazines named Palouse Ridge the "Best New Course" and PNW Golfer Magazine cited the 15th hole as one of the "Best Holes of the Northwest".

All green fees include a cart. Monday thru Thursday local residents pay $55 for 18 holes and non-residents pay $99. Seniors age 60 and older can play for $45. Juniors age 16 and younger pay $20. When space is open anyone can play Friday thru Sunday and on holidays. Students pay $40 Monday thru Thursday and $50 weekends and holidays. WSU members play for $55.

They have a clubhouse, putting greens, chipping and pitching areas, pro shop, 36-tee driving range and banquet facilities. Lessons and help with tournament planning is available. They charge $5-10 for a bucket of balls.

Directions: On the northeast side of the WSU campus. Take Main Street to Airport Road and head north 2 miles to the course.

Quincy

Colockum Ridge Golf Course

18 Holes ◇ Par 71 ◇ Length 5895 yards ◇ $-$$

17056 Road 5 NW ◇ Quincy, WA

509-787-6026

www.colockumridgegolf.com

The Colockum Ridge course has three sets of tees. From the forward tees the total distance is 5150 yards. The slope is 101 and the course rating 67.3 on this Bill Tuefel designed golf course. Open year round, this is an easy-to-walk course with enough challenge for all levels.

Weekend green fees are $20 for 9 or $30 for 18. During the week it's $15 and $25. The non-holiday Monday Special is $13-15. Golf clubs rent for $10-12, pull carts for $5 and motorized carts are $10 per seat.

Facilities include a restaurant and pro shop. Lessons and help with tournament planning are available at the pro shop.

Directions: On Highway 281 at its junction with Road 5 NW located about halfway between I-90 freeway and Quincy, 5 miles south of town.

Crescent Bar Resort Golf Course

9 Holes ◇ Par 35 ◇ Length 3034 yards ◇ $-$$

8894 Crescent Bar Road NW ◇ Quincy, WA

509-787-1511 ◇ Reservations Available

www.crescentbarresort.com

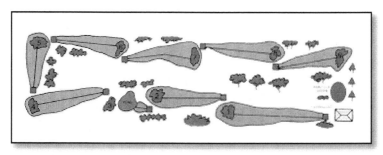

Crescent Bar Resort is situated on the Columbia River and the scenery is gorgeous. The golf course is surrounded on three sides by the river. The fairways are pretty straight, the greens well maintained and hazards consist of one pond, some trees and the Columbia River. From the ladies' tees the total distance is 2844 yards for a par of 36. The slope for this course is 118 and the rating 68.4.

Friday thru Sunday 9 holes will cost you $23 and 18 are $28. The rest of the week you'll pay $14 and $18. Seniors age 62 and older can play on non-holiday Mondays for $14 and $18. Juniors age 11 and younger pay the same rate every day between noon and 5:00 pm. Clubs rent for $10 or $15 and power carts $10 per person for 9 or $15 per person if 18. The trail fee for your own cart is $5.

The resort offers lodging, convention facilities, a restaurant/lounge with banquet facilities, putting green and driving range. The driving range has grass tees and charges $4 for a bucket of balls. Tournament planning help is available and lessons too. Ask at the pro shop.

Directions: From Quincy take Highway 28 towards Wenatchee and after 7 miles turn left on Crescent Bar Road. The course is 3 miles further.

Sunserra Golf Course

9 Holes ◇ Par 27 ◇ Length 1205 yards ◇ $-$$

23572 Sunserra Loop Road ◇ Quincy, WA

509-787-4156 ◇ Reservations Available

www.sunserra.com

This semi-private course was built in 2006, has large greens, lots of bunkers and plenty of water. Each hole has a gorgeous view of the Columbia River.

This par 3 course has homes on one side and the river on the other. It was designed by Raven Fontenot and has undulating greens and is challenging yet good for a casual game too. From the forward tees the total distance is 1040 yards.

Green fees Friday thru Sunday are $20 for 9 holes or $25 for 18. Monday thru Thursday you'll pay $15 and $20. On Monday's seniors age 60 and older pay $10 for 9 holes or $15 for 18.

Golf clubs rent for $5, pull carts $3 and motorized carts are $10 per person.

Sunserra is part of a golf community with some vacation rentals, a nice restaurant and lounge, snack bar, putting green and chipping area.

Directions: Located at the Crescent Bar Resort, on the Columbia River. From Quincy take Highway 28 towards Wenatchee. After 7 miles turn left onto Crescent Bar Road. The golf course is 3 miles further. Follow the Sunserra signs.

Richland

Buckskin Golf Club

9 Holes <> Par 34
Length 2535 yards <> $

1790 Bronco Lane
Richland, WA

509-942-0888
Reservations Available

Buckskin opened in 1999 and was designed by Jeff Marcum. The slope is 97 and the rating 31.2. It is flat with a few trees and natural brush boundaries. From the forward tees the total distance is 2100 yards.

The signature hole requires you to shoot between two trees. Small greens and a challenging desert surface will make you work for par.

Green fees remain the same seven days a week all year long. You'll pay $14 for 9 holes or $20 for 18. Juniors and seniors can play for $12 and $14.

Golf clubs rent for $10, pull carts are $3 and motorized carts $10 per person for 9 holes or $15 per person on 18.

Facilities include a 25-tee driving range, limited pro shop and a banquet area. At the pro shop they can arrange lessons and help with tournament planning.

On the driving range a bucket of balls will cost $3-6 depending on the size bucket. Cold drinks are available.

Directions: Located 2 miles northwest of downtown. You'll find the road just beyond Van Giesen Street's junction with Highway 240.

Columbia Point Golf Course

9 Holes ◇ Par 37 ◇ Length 3506 yards ◇ $$-$$$

225 Columbia Point Drive ◇ Richland, WA

509-946-0710 ◇ Reservations Available

www.playcolumbiapoint.com

This city-owned course opened in 1997 and is suitable for all levels of golfers. Designed by James Engh, the terrain features rolling fairways and large undulating greens. From the red tees the distance is 2592 yards.

Green fees are $27 for 9 holes or $48 for 18 on weekends and holidays. On Fridays you'll pay $27 and $43, and on Monday thru Thursday $23 and $38. Discount rates begin 5 hours before sunset and drop again 2 hours later. Those super twilight rates are $23 or go earlier and you'll pay $30-40 depending on the day of the week.

Clubs rent for $9 and $18 and pull carts are $2 and $3. Motorized carts are $8 per person for 9 holes or $13.50 for 18.

Seniors age 55 and older can play Monday thru Thursday for $21 and $30, after 1:00 pm on Fridays for $21 and $36, or on weekends for $30 and $41. Juniors age 16 and younger can play Monday thru Thursday for $14 and $20, and after 1:00 pm Friday thru Sunday for $16 and $25.

Facilities include putting and chipping greens, a practice bunker, a full-service pro shop, a cafe with a full bar, clubhouse and driving range.

At the 20-grass-tee driving range you can get a small bucket of balls for $4, large is $6 and extra-large $8. They are open dawn to dusk. You can arrange for private or group lessons and get help with tournament planning at the pro shop.

Directions: Located just off George Washington Way and I-182.

Horn Rapids Golf Course

18 Holes <> Par 72 <> Length 7060 yards <> $$-$$$

2800 Horn Rapids Drive <> Richland, WA

509-375-4714 <> Reservations Available

www.hornrapidsgolf.com

Horn Rapids was built in 1993 and will make you feel like you're playing in the middle of nowhere. It's a target-style course, the only one of its kind in Eastern Washington. You'll find no trees, just lots of desert roughs. The terrain is rolling and water comes into play on the 9th and 18th holes.

Open year round weather permitting from 7:00 am to dusk, the slope is 139 and the course rating 74.0. They offer four sets of tees. The total distance from the forward tees is 4367 yards.

Green fees Monday thru Thursday are $22 for 9 holes or $37 for 18 all year long. On Fridays they charge $25 and $42. Weekends and holidays the rates are $25 and $47 May thru mid-November and $22 and $45 the balance of the year. Twilight rates begin at 2:00 pm. You'll pay $38 May thru mid-November and $35 the balance of the year.

You can rent golf clubs for $10, pull carts $5 and power carts $11 and $15. They have a full-service pro shop, an 18-hole putting course, a driving range and snack bar.

The Mirage Putting Course at Horn Rapids charges $5 for adults and $4 for youngsters. Lessons and help with tournament planning are available at the pro shop.

Directions: Located 4 miles northwest of downtown via Highway 240.

Ritzville

Ritzville Golf Course

9 Holes ◇ Par 35 ◇ Length 2821 yards ◇ $-$$

104 E 10th Street ◇ Ritzville, WA

509-659-9868

The Ritzville municipal course is open mid-February thru mid-November from 8:00 am to 8:00 pm. Built in 1940, it has narrow fairways, tall trees and small fast greens. This course has a slope of 122 and a rating of 36.4. From the ladies' tees par is 36.

Play early in the day in late summer and avoid the heat. This course operates on the honor system the balance of the year.

Green fees during the week are $14 for 9 holes or $20 for 18. On weekends and holidays you'll pay $16 or $22. Monday thru Friday unless it's a holiday students can play for $5. Seniors age 55 and older pay $12 for 9 holes or $17 for 18.

On Mondays anyone can play all day for $25. Twilight rates begin two hours before dark and everyone pays $8. After mid-November this course operates on the honor system. You can play by depositing $5 in the honor box so bring exact change.

Facilities include a putting green, a restaurant where you'll find cold beer, plus a banquet area and a full-service pro shop.

Directions: Located right in Ritzville on 10th Street.

Royal City

Royal City Golf Course

9 Holes ◇ Par 36 ◇ Length 3106 yards ◇ $-$$

13702 Dodson Road S ◇ Royal City, WA

509-346-2052

Royal City opened in 1991 and is a year-round course that only closes for severe weather. You'll find rolling fairways, water on two holes and bent grass greens. The women's tees have a distance of 2850 yards.

Two sets of tees are available. The signature hole is a 406 yard shot taken over a pond. The slope is 127 and the rating 72.1.

On Mondays and Tuesdays you can golf all day at Royal City for $15. Wednesday thru Friday you'll pay $15 for 9 holes or $20 for 18. On weekends and holidays the rates are $15 and $25.

Seniors age 65 and older save $2 off green fees Wednesday thru Sunday, and kids younger than 12 play for half price.

Clubs rent for $4 and $6, pull carts $4 and motorized carts are $8 per seat on 9 holes or $10 per seat on 18. The trail fee if you bring your own motorized cart is $3-5.

The pro shop is limited but they offer snacks and cold pop as well as help with tournament planning and lessons. They have an RV park and a driving range too.

Directions: This course is located at the corner of Highway 26 and Dodson Road, east of Royal City.

Spokane

Downriver Golf Course

18 Holes ◇ Par 71 ◇ Length 6130 yards ◇ $$

3225 Columbia Circle ◇ Spokane, WA

509-327-5269 ◇ Reservations Available

www.golfdownriver.org

The Downriver Golf Course has narrow fairways, some trees, a few sand traps, lots of hills and some pretty good par 3's. Weather permitting they are open 6:00 am to dark April thru October. The course offers three sets of tees. From the women's tees the total distance is 5592 yards for a par of 73. Built in 1916 this course has mature trees and sits along the Spokane River.

Green fees are $22 for 9 holes or $31 for 18. Monday thru Thursday. Friday thru Sunday and on holidays you'll pay $22 to play 9 or $34 for 18 holes. Juniors pay $10 all week long. For $37 you can buy a discount card that lets you play for reduced rates. Motorized carts rent for $15 per person per 9 holes.

Facilities include a restaurant/lounge that serves beer and wine, plus banquet rooms, a full-service pro shop and a driving range. Lessons and help with tournament planning are available at the pro shop.

Directions: Take the Maple Toll Bridge exit off I-90, turn left at Northwest Boulevard and after the third stoplight turn left again onto Euclid Avenue. Follow the Downriver Golf Course signs from there.

Esmeralda Golf Course

18 Holes ◇ Par 70 ◇ Length 6249 yards ◇ $$

3933 E Courtland ◇ Spokane, WA

509-487-6261 ◇ Reservations Available

www.esmeraldagolf.org

Esmeralda Golf Course is a joy to play all year long with its rolling hills and beautiful maples but you'll need good putting skills to break par.

The course opens every year in mid-February and closes in mid-November. Built in 1956, the women's tees have a total distance of 5600 yards for a par of 72.

This is a good course for all levels of play with its easy-to-walk fairways and over 2,000 mature trees.

Green fees at Esmeralda are $22 for 9 holes or $31 for 18 holes Monday thru Thursday. Friday thru Sunday and on holidays you'll pay $22 for 9 holes or $34 for 18 holes. Juniors pay $10. For $37 anyone can buy an annual discount card that lets them play for reduced rates.

Motorized carts are $15 per person for 9 holes and facilities at Esmeralda Golf Course include a restaurant that serves beer and wine, a pro shop and driving range.

Directions: Go north on Division to Wellesey, turn right and go to Freya, turn right again, heading south to Courtland and turn left to the course.

Hangman Valley Golf Course

18 Holes ◇ Par 72 ◇ Length 6865 yards ◇ $$

2210 E Hangman Valley Road ◇ Spokane, WA

509-448-1212 ◇ Reservations Available

Hangman Valley is open from mid-March to early November weather permitting. The terrain is rolling with lots of trees and fairly open fairways. It's a challenging, well-trapped course with medium-sized greens and some water.

They offer three sets of tees. The women's s tees have a total distance of 5699 yards for a par of 71. Designed by Bob and Robert Baldock, this course opened in 1969. It was renovated in 2008.

Monday thru Thursday you'll pay $22 for 9 holes or $30 for 18. Before 3:00 pm Friday thru Sunday and on all holidays green fees are $28 and $34. After 3:00 pm you'll pay $28 whether you play 9 holes or 18.

Seven days a week juniors can play 9 holes for $9 or 18 holes for $15. A $30 discount card will save you lots of money if you play Spokane County courses very often.

Hangman Valley has a driving range where floating balls are hit into a lake. Course facilities include a full-service pro shop and a restaurant and lounge with banquet facilities. You can get help with tournament planning and arrange for golf lessons at the pro shop.

Directions: Leave I-90 on Highway 195, go 4.5 miles to Hatch Road, turn left then right onto Hangman Valley Road and drive 4.5 miles to the course.

Indian Canyon Golf Course

18 Holes ◇ Par 72 ◇ Length 6296 yards ◇ $$

W 4304 West Drive ◇ Spokane, WA

509-747-5353

www.my.spokanecity.org/golf/courses/indian-canyon

You'll find this course at the top of Sunset Hill. It first opened in 1935. The terrain is hilly and the course open from March thru October. It overlooks the city of Spokane and 3 sets of tees offer variety. From the women's tees the distance is 5318 yards for a par of 73. Indian Canyon was designed by Chandler Egan, the same man who designed Pebble Beach. It is built on a canyon wall with a 240' drop and has lots of big trees.

Green fees at Indian Canyon are $22 for 9 holes or $31 for 18 Monday thru Thursday. Friday thru Sunday and on holidays you'll pay $22 to play 9 or $34 for 18 holes. Juniors pay $10. For $37 you can buy a discount card that lets you play for reduced rates. Motorized carts are $15 per person per 9 holes.

Facilities include a driving range, a restaurant and lounge with banquet facilities and a limited pro shop where you can get help with tournament planning and arrange for lessons.

Directions: Leave I-90 at the Garden Springs exit and follow the signs.

Painted Hills Golf Course

18 Holes ◇ Par 36 ◇ Length 3382 yards ◇ $-$$

S 4403 Dishman-Mica Road ◇ Spokane, WA

509-928-4653

There are two 9-hole golf courses here, a par 36 Championship Course and the Chester Creek Par 3. Both are easy to walk and open year round, weather permitting. On the Championship Course you'll find an interesting flat terrain with water on four holes and white-sand traps. The forward tees have a total distance of 2562 yards.

The par 3 Chester Creek course is great for families and beginners but even more advanced players will enjoy this short course. The holes range from 52 yards to 120 yards in length presenting more experienced golfers with a chance to work on their short game.

Green fees on the **Championship Course** Monday thru Thursday are $10 for 9 holes or $18 for 18. The rest of the week you'll pay $18 and $24. Seniors age 60 and older play for $14 and $18 early in the week. They pay $12 and $18 Friday thru Sunday. Juniors age 17 and younger pay $10 and $13 Monday thru Thursday and $12 and $18 Friday thru Sunday. Motorized carts rent for $6 per rider for 9 holes.

On the **Chester Creek Par 3** green fees are the same seven days a week, $10 for 9 holes, $13 for 18 or $15 to play all day. Juniors and seniors pay $7, $10 and $13.

Facilities include a restaurant that serves beer and wine, plus a lighted driving range and a full-service pro shop. The driving range has 36 mat tees and a multi-tiered grass tee and is open until 10:00 pm April thru September. You can get 45 balls for $5, 75 for $7 and 115 for $8 at the driving range.

Directions: From I-90 take the Argonne exit #287 and head south 5 miles to the golf course.

Pine Acres Par 3

9 Holes ◇ Par 27 ◇ Length 760 yards ◇ $

11912 N Division Street ◇ Spokane, WA

509-466-9984

www.pineacresgolf.com

Pine Acres was built in 1960 and is open March thru October. The terrain is flat and easy to walk. It's a good place for beginners and those looking to practice their short game.

Green fees are $9 for 9 holes or $13 for 18 holes all week long. Juniors and seniors save $1 off regular rates.

You'll find practice greens and traps, a discount golf shop, snacks, cold drinks and a driving range here. Lessons are given during the summer. At the driving range you can get a bucket of balls for $6.50 to $10 depending on how many balls you need.

Directions: Located 7 miles north of downtown Spokane. Leave Highway 395 at Division Street. The course is located next to Fred Meyers.

The Creek at Qualchan

18 Holes ◇ Par 72 ◇ Length 6577 yards ◇ $$

301 E Meadow Lane ◇ Spokane, WA

509-448-9317 ◇ Reservations Available

www.my.spokanecity.org/golf/courses/qualchan

You play across the creek five times at Qualchan. Its front nine is flat with some rolling hills. The back nine is tree lined and hilly. In all 5 ponds and 65 bunkers are found and the scenery is spectacular. There are four sets of tees and the forward tees have a distance of 5535 yards. The course is open March thru November from 7:00 am to dusk. This natural setting serves as a sanctuary for local birds and wildlife.

Green fees are $22 for 9 holes or $31 for 18 Monday thru Thursday. Friday thru Sunday and on holidays you'll pay $22 or $34. Juniors pay $13. For $37 you can buy a card that lets you play for reduced rates.

Motorized carts are $15 per person per 9 holes. You'll find a restaurant with banquet facilities, cold beer and wine plus a driving range and a full-service pro shop. Lessons and help with tournament planning are available.

Directions: Leave I-90 on Hwy. 195 south. Course is 5 minutes from downtown Spokane.

Wandermere Golf Course

18 Holes ◇ Par 70 ◇ Length 6050 yards ◇ $-$$

13700 N Division Street ◇ Spokane, WA

509-466-8023 ◇ Reservations Available

www.wandermere.com

Hole	1	2	3	4	5	6	7	8	9	Out	10	11	12	13	14	15	16	17	18	In	Total
Blue	375	150	380	375	165	400	520	355	325	3,045	415	335	405	470	135	325	405	150	365	3,005	6,050
White	360	140	340	365	155	340	470	310	310	2,790	405	325	395	400	125	315	405	140	325	2,835	5,625
Men's Handicap	3	15	9	11	13	7	1	5	17		8	14	4	2	18	16	6	12	10		
Men's Par	4	3	4	4	3	4	5	4	4	35	4	4	4	5	3	4	4	3	4	35	70
Women's Par	4	3	4	4	3	4	5	4	4	35	5	4	4	5	3	4	4	3	4	36	71
Women's Handicap	3	15	7	9	11	5	1	13	17		8	14	6	2	18	16	4	10	12		
Red	360	120	315	335	155	330	415	300	295	2,625	405	315	355	360	125	305	315	125	275	2,580	5,205

Wandermere has some of the toughest holes in the city. Built in 1929 it has a rolling terrain. When playing 18 holes you have to shoot across a river twice and around three ponds. The slope is 113 and the course rating 68.5. Open March thru October from 5:00 am to dusk. The distance from the forward tees is 5625 yards.

During the week you can play 9 holes for $19 or 18 for $25. On weekends you pay $29 whether you play 9 holes or 18. Seniors age 60 and older pay $16 for 9 holes or $21 for 18 Monday thru Friday. Juniors age 17 and younger pay $18 on weekdays whether playing 9 or 18 holes.

Golf clubs rent for $10, pull carts are $4 and motorized carts $15 per 9 holes. The trail fee if you bring your own motorized cart is $7.

Facilities include a restaurant/lounge with a banquet area, plus a full service pro shop and driving range. Lessons are available as is help with tournament planning.

Directions: Located 8.6 miles north of downtown Spokane. Follow Division Street north. The course is located just past Hastings Road.

St. John

St. John Golf & Country Club
9 Holes ◇ Par 35 ◇ Length 2700 yards ◇ $
232 Lancaster Highway ◇ St. John, WA
509-648-3259 ◇ Reservations Available

The St. John Golf Club course had only 6 holes for many years. In 1995 it officially became a 9-hole golf course. The terrain is flat, the course well-maintained and the fairways are lined with trees. The greens are small and the course interesting. You'll find a dogleg on the 4th hole that requires you to shoot over water onto a narrow landing spot for a par 4.

No matter when you play green fees at the St. John course are $15. Pull carts rent for $3 and motorized carts are $25.

They have a full-service pro shop, snack bar, practice green and a driving range. You'll find help with tournament planning at the pro shop.

Directions: Located right in St. John along Highway 23.

Sunnyside

Black Rock Creek Golf Club

18 Holes ◇ Par 72 ◇ Length 6700 yards ◇ $

31 Ray Road ◇ Sunnyside, WA

509-837-5340 ◇ Reservations Available

www.blackrockcreekgc.com

This course is open year round and over half the holes have water. The slope is 112, the rating 70.2 and it has more than 40 sand traps. You'll find three sets of tees. The front tees are 5500 yards.

March thru September green fees are $18 for 9 or $33 for 18 holes on weekends. On weekdays you'll pay $16 and $29. The rest of the year it's $12 and $20 during the week or $15 and $25 on weekends.

Motorized carts are $8 and $14 per person. They have a pro shop, snack bar, practice green, driving range and provide help with tournament planning and lessons. At the driving range they charge $2-4 for a bucket of balls.

Directions: Southeast of downtown Sunnyside. Located just east of I-82.

Tekoa

Tekoa Golf & Country Club

9 Holes ◇ Par 35 ◇ Length 2550 yards ◇ $-$$

Golf Course Road at Highway 27 ◇ Tekoa, WA

509-284-5607

www.tekoacc.com

The Tekoa Golf and Country Club is a semi-private course and open April thru October. Built in 1959, it offers nice greens, a semi-hilly terrain and excellent views of the surrounding fields and mountains. The designer was Waldo Hay. The slope is 111 and the course rating 34.4. Tekoa offers country golf at its best, not over-manicured links.

Weekday green fees are $16 for 9 holes or $29 for 18. On weekends it's $20 and $34. Seniors play on non-holiday weekdays for $20. Juniors pay $9 and $15 during the week and $15 and $18 on weekends. If you have ID showing you are active military or a college student it's $14 and $22 during the week.

Clubs rent for $3, handcarts are $5 and motorized carts $11 per seat for 9 holes or $16 per seat on 18. When the course is not staffed simply put your fees in the honor box. Be sure to bring exact change. Facilities on season include a restaurant and a limited pro shop.

Directions: From town head south .5 mile on Farmington Highway.

Walla Walla

Veterans Memorial Golf Course

18 Holes ◇ Par 72 ◇ Length 6646 yards ◇ $$

201 E Rees ◇ Walla Walla, WA

509-527-4507 ◇ Reservations Available

www.vetsmemorialgolf.com

This semi-private course is short, tight, interesting and has fast greens. Open year round, the course rating is 70.7 and the slope 115. The terrain is fairly

218

flat and the total distance from the red tees 5403 yards. Located in the foothills of the Blue Mountains and part of Walla Walla's living memorial to war veterans, this course first opened in 1948.

Seven days a week you'll pay $23 for 9 holes or $35 for 18. Seniors pay $19 for 9 holes or $29 for 18. Juniors 17 and younger pay $9 and $15. Those with student identification age 18-25 can play 9 holes for only $12.

Facilities include a clubhouse, a restaurant and lounge with banquet facilities, a 25-tee driving range and a pro shop where you can get help with lessons and tournament planning.

Directions: Leave Highway 410 at the second exit and follow the signs.

Wine Valley Golf Club

18 Holes ◇ Par 72 ◇ Length 7360 yards ◇ $$$-$$$$

201 E Rees ◇ Walla Walla, WA

877-333-9842 ◇ Reservations Available

www.winevalleygolfclub.com

This semi-private links-style golf course has plenty of water, and terrific views of the Blue Mountains. Designed by Dan Hixson, the course has 5 sets of tees. The distance from the ladies' tees is 5105 yards. The Wine Valley course slope is 130 and the rating 75.5. The fairways are wide with lots of bunkers.

Green fees are for 18 holes and the highest during May thru September. You'll pay $95 Monday thru Thursday and $110 Friday thru Sunday and all major holidays. The Twilight Rate is $75 during the week and $90 on weekends. At 5:00 pm it drops to $50 seven days a week.

They are cheapest November thru February when Monday thru Thursday you'll pay $50. Friday thru Sunday and on holidays you'll pay $65. During March, April and October it will cost you $60 and $75. Seniors get a $10 discount Monday thru Thursday. Qualifying juniors save $20. Motorized carts are $30.

Directions: Follow Second Avenue for 1 mile and turn right on East Rees Avenue.

Warden

Sage Hills Golf Club

18 Holes <> Par 71 <> Length 6591 yards <> $

10400 Sage Hills Road SE <> Warden, WA

509-349-2603 <> Reservations Available

www.sagehills.com

Sage Hills is open February thru November weather permitting from 6:00 am to dusk. It's a well maintained course with four sets of tees and large greens. The distance from the women's tees is 5665 yards for a par of 74.

Located in the heart of the Columbia Basin this course is surrounded by sand and sagebrush. The terrain is gently rolling and has enough water and sand hazards to keep you on your toes. The slope is 122 and the course rating 74.2.

On weekends you'll pay $24 for 9 holes or $33 for 18. During the week it's $19 and $30. Seniors age 62 and older pay $13 and $20 Monday thru Friday. Juniors age 7 to 16 pay $12 and $17. Twilight rates begin at 2:00 pm and everyone pays $20 seven days a week. Golf clubs rent for $8 and $12, pull carts are $3 and $6, and motorized carts are $12 per person.

Facilities include a restaurant and lounge, banquet facilities, a full-service pro shop, RV park and a driving range. Lessons and help with tournament planning are available at the pro shop.

Directions: Located 7.3 miles northwest of Warden via Highway 170 and Highway 17.

West Richland

West Richland Golf Course

18 Holes ◇ Par 71 ◇ Length 5987 yards ◇ $

4000 Fallon Drive ◇ West Richland, WA

509-967-2165 ◇ Reservations Available

www.westrichlandgolf.com

This challenging year-round course is right in West Richland. The terrain is fairly flat and easy to walk and the course borders the Yakima River on one side. The greens are small and the total distance from the women's tees is 5800 yards. This course can be played in less than 4 hours.

Monday thru Thursday green fees are $14 for 9 holes or $19 for 18. Friday thru Sunday and on all major holidays you'll pay $15 and $26. Seniors age 55 and older can play Monday thru Thursday for $13 and $17. Juniors play for $12 and $17. Twilight begins 4 hours before dusk and is $25 per person including the cart. Golf clubs rent for $5 per 9 holes, pull carts are $2 and $3, and motorized carts $13 per 9 holes.

Facilities include a new clubhouse, a restaurant and lounge with banquet facilities plus a full-service pro shop and driving range. At the driving range you'll pay $3, $5 or $7 depending on how many balls you need. Lessons and tournament planning can be arranged. Ask at the pro shop.

Directions: From Bypass 240 take the Van Giesen NW exit, turn right onto 38th Street and follow this to the course. The total distance is about 1 mile.

Wilbur

Big Bend Golf Club

9 Holes <> Par 36 <> Length 2985 yards <> $

Highway 2 at Highway 174 <> Wilbur, WA

509-647-5664 <> Reservations Advised

www.bigbendgolfandcountryclub.com

Built in 1964 the Big Bend course is considered one of the best 9-hole courses in eastern Washington. It offers excellent greens, sand bunkers and some hills. The slope is 107 for men and 120 for women. The ratings are 64.7 and 73.6. Open March thru November weather permitting the women's par is 37 for a total distance of 2875 yards.

On weekends and holidays you'll pay $20 for 9 holes or $26 for 18. During the week it's $16 and $22. Monday thru Friday seniors age 65 and older play for $11 and $16. Juniors age 17 and younger pay $8 and $13. Clubs rent for $6, pull carts $3 and motorized carts are $12. Bring your own cart and the trail fee is $7 per day.

Facilities include a lounge where liquor is served plus a snack bar, banquet area and driving range. At the range you'll find grass tees and can get a bucket of balls for $2-4 depending on how many you need. Lessons and help with tournament planning are available; ask at the pro shop.

Directions: Located at the west end of Wilber, at the junction of Highways 2 and 174.

INDEX

N

M

O

U

T

V

GOLF BOOKS BY KIKI CANNIFF

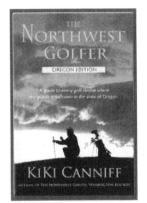

THE NORTHWEST GOLFER provides Oregon and Washington golfers with a quick and easy way to locate every golf course in the Pacific Northwest where the public is welcome.

Golfers in Oregon and Washington can play on courses designed by famous architects, tee off in the shadow of gorgeous snow-capped mountains, and hone their skills on some pretty unique terrain.

The Northwest Golfer provides golfers with an easy way to keep the region's more than 350 public golf courses at their fingertips. There is one volume for Oregon golfers and another one for those in Washington.

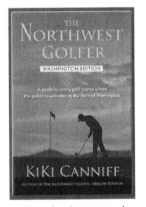

Both books are laid out in an identical format with each state divided into four vertical sections. Cities and courses are then listed alphabetically.

Each listing begins with a handy reference line that reveals the course's yardage, par, number of holes and price range. This is followed by contact information, along with details about the course terrain, designer, history, facilities available, green fees, equipment rental rates, discount times and more.

Golfers in Oregon or Washington have enjoyed The Northwest Golfer for decades; it was first published in 1986 and updated when needed.

www.OneMorePress.com

Made in the USA
San Bernardino, CA
13 June 2016